PLAY IT AGAIN, SAM

by Terence Reese
and Martin Hoffman

Published by
Devyn Press, Inc.
Louisville, Kentucky

Cover by Bonnie Baron Pollack

Devyn Press, Inc.
151 Thierman Lane
Louisville, KY 40207

ISBN 0-910791-21-X

Table of Contents

1 Double Void..5
2 Informative Double 7
3 Lion's Den 9
4 Objection Overruled 11
5 Losing Option 15
6 Always Time 19
7 Unlucky Decision 22
8 Spare Man 26
9 Finesse Not Needed..............................29
10 A Delicate Affair 31
11 Wrong Track 33
12 The Strangler 36
13 Lofty Answer 39
14 The Luck Was There 41
15 Not A Guess 43
16 Collapse of Stout Party 45
17 Medal Chance 47
18 Disappearing Trick 49
19 Two-Two To Tooting 51
20 Backstage 53
21 Blind Alley..55
22 Non-Trier 57
23 Just An Idea 59
24 A Slight Difference 63
25 Other Way Up 65
26 Don't Stop!..67
27 On The Right Side...............................69
28 No Hurry 71
29 Reputation Missed 73
30 High Branches 77
31 Outbid And Outplayed...........................79
32 Wrong Exit..81
33 A Question Of Control 83

34 Optical Illusion...................................85
35 Still Asleep......................................87
36 False Encouragement..............................89
37 Through The Slips.................................91
38 Next Round 93
39 Different Mistake.................................95
40 Taking The Cue...................................99
41 Force Of Habit..................................101
42 Partial Recovery................................103
43 More Trouble....................................105
44 Remove The Obstruction..........................107
45 Test Case 109
46 Slight Hazard...................................111
47 Eye On The Ball 113
48 Not Unexpected..................................115
49 Nothing To Spare 117
50 Awkward Moment.................................121
51 Second Choice 123
52 Hippo Dancing...................................125
53 Early Surrender 127
54 Happy Ending 129
55 They Missed It...................................131
56 Jack In The Box 134
57 Jaws 137
58 Cut And Run 139
59 Seeking Information..............................141
60 He Resigned Too Soon 144
61 Interesting Exercise 147
62 Foolish Intervention.............................149
63 A Chance To Impress 151
64 South Strikes Back...............................155
65 On The Wrong Side 157

Foreword

There is a general belief that the technique of play is fairly well understood. Safety play, communication play, elimination play, squeeze play — these are the familiar headings in innumerable books, to which I have made my own contribution. It is sometimes said that the game is more or less "written out."

An exceptional player such as Martin Hoffman, who plays with dozens of different partners and is a favourite for every big event he enters, has shown that this is far from being the case. He makes notes of interesting deals he has played or defended, and on this occasion he has asked me to collaborate with him in presenting some of these. We have used what I think is a new formula: the hands are played in the way that a good player would tackle them, and then the omniscient North points out what might have been a better line of play.

If I may add a word of advice to the reader: don't read how the hand was played by South and think, "Well, that seems reasonable, I wonder what North is going to suggest," and then turn the page. Work at each hand, decide what was wrong with the declarer's line of play. You won't always be right, but in a short while your game will improve beyond recognition.

Terence Reese

1 DOUBLE VOID

Dealer East
Neither side vulnerable

```
              ♠ K 10 8 7 6
              ♡ A 2
              ◇ 10 3
              ♣ K 10 9 6
♡J led            N
              W       E
                  S
              ♠ J 2
              ♡ K Q 6 5
              ◇ Q 8 7 5
              ♣ A Q 4
```

South	West	North	East
			1 ◇
Pass	1 ♡	1 ♠	3 ◇
3 NT	Pass	Pass	Pass

South's 3 NT was a bold venture to obtain a good score in a pairs event.

West led the ♡J, East discarding a diamond. South won with the king and finessed the ♠J, losing to the queen. East played off ace, king and jack of diamonds. The clubs broke, but South could take only three hearts, one diamond and four clubs before losing the lead to East, who still had the ♠A and a winning diamond. The defence made two spades and three diamonds.

"I could have doubled 3 ◇," said South, "but I thought we might score well in 3 NT."

"There were eight tricks on top," said North, "with the ♣J coming down. You should have been able to manage a ninth, especially as you knew early that West was void of diamonds and East of hearts."

Replay of 1

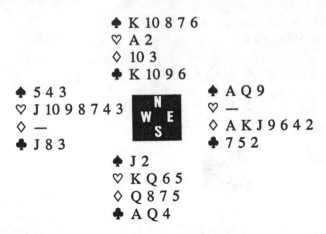

```
                    ♠ K 10 8 7 6
                    ♡ A 2
                    ♢ 10 3
                    ♣ K 10 9 6
 ♠ 5 4 3                              ♠ A Q 9
 ♡ J 10 9 8 7 4 3      N              ♡ —
 ♢ —                 W   E            ♢ A K J 9 6 4 2
 ♣ J 8 3               S              ♣ 7 5 2
                    ♠ J 2
                    ♡ K Q 6 5
                    ♢ Q 8 7 5
                    ♣ A Q 4
```

South played in 3 NT after East had shown length in diamonds and West in hearts. When West led the ♡J, South won with the king and ran the ♠J. East won and played off ace, king and jack of diamonds. South could run only eight tricks before losing the lead to East, who held two more winners.

"You can expect to make four tricks in clubs sooner or later," said North. "That gives you eight on top. Surely the game is to bring pressure on East in spades and diamonds. Instead of taking the spade finesse run three hearts and four clubs. This brings you to:

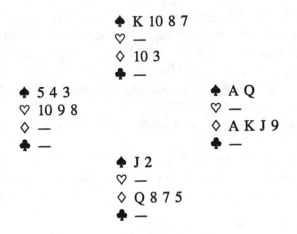

```
                    ♠ K 10 8 7
                    ♡ —
                    ♢ 10 3
                    ♣ —
 ♠ 5 4 3                              ♠ A Q
 ♡ 10 9 8                             ♡ —
 ♢ —                                  ♢ A K J 9
 ♣ —                                  ♣ —
                    ♠ J 2
                    ♡ —
                    ♢ Q 8 7 5
                    ♣ —
```

"You lead a diamond from dummy and make two more tricks."

2 INFORMATIVE DOUBLE

Dealer North
North - South vulnerable

```
              ♠ K 10 2
              ♡ A Q 10 5
              ◇ Q 10 7 6
              ♣ A 10

  ♣5 led         N
              W     E
                 S

              ♠ A Q J 9 8
              ♡ 2
              ◇ A 9
              ♣ K Q 9 8 3
```

South	West	North	East
		1 ◇	Pass
1 ♠	Pass	1 NT	Pass
3 ♣	Pass	4 ♠	Pass
6 ♠	Pass	Pass	Double
Pass	Pass	Pass	

North - South were playing a weak notrump throughout and North's rebid of 1 NT was in the 15-16 range.

West led a low club and dummy's 10 was ruffed by East, who returned a trump. All followed to a second round of trumps, so there was a spade left in dummy for the fifth club. The declarer tried to establish an extra heart trick, playing West for J x x, but this failed and in the end he had to lose a diamond.

"Unlucky, but I don't think you gave it the best play," said North. "East was likely to hold a void in clubs and strength in both red suits, wasn't he? If you take that into consideration you have a chance. In fact, you can make it."

Replay of 2

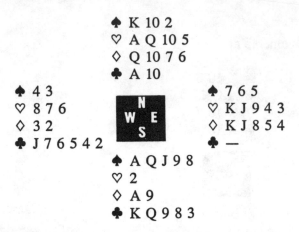

```
                ♠ K 10 2
                ♡ A Q 10 5
                ◇ Q 10 7 6
                ♣ A 10
  ♠ 4 3                          ♠ 7 6 5
  ♡ 8 7 6          N             ♡ K J 9 4 3
  ◇ 3 2         W     E          ◇ K J 8 5 4
  ♣ J 7 6 5 4 2    S             ♣ —
                ♠ A Q J 9 8
                ♡ 2
                ◇ A 9
                ♣ K Q 9 8 3
```

South played in 6♠ doubled after North had opened 1◇. South had bid spades and clubs, and East's double was evidently a request for an unusual lead. He ruffed the club lead and returned a trump. South was able to draw the remaining trumps in two rounds, but had to lose a trick in the red suits.

"As the cards lie, I think you can do it if you go up with the ♣A," said North. "East ruffs, as expected, and returns a trump. But now you can draw two trumps, ruff a club, killing West's jack, and return to the ◇A. You play off the rest of the trumps, keeping the ♡A Q in dummy, the ♡2 and the ◇9 in your own hand. Not easy, I agree, but if you assume the club lead is going to be ruffed, your position is more fluid if you play the ace from dummy."

3   LION'S DEN

Dealer North
Neither side vulnerable

```
            ♠ 2
            ♡ A 3
            ◇ K 9 8 7
            ♣ K Q J 10 7 6
```

♠ A led

```
         N
      W     E
         S
```

```
            ♠ 5 4
            ♡ Q 8 7 6
            ◇ Q J 10 6 5
            ♣ 5 2
```

South	West	North	East
		1♣	Double
1◇	1♠	3◇	4♠
Pass	Pass	5◇	Pass
Pass	Double	Pass	Pass
Pass			

Playing in a pairs event, North took the view that the save in 5 ◇ was unlikely to cost more than 300. However, West led the ♠ A and East played the queen, inviting a switch to hearts. West led a heart at trick two and South went up with the ace. East won the first diamond, cashed the ♡ K, led a club to the ace and ruffed a club. That was 500 to the defence and a poor result for North - South.

"Not much sense in bidding 3 ◇ and following with 5 ◇, is there?" demanded South, who felt that on this occasion he was blameless.

"One has to do that sort of thing sometimes in pairs play," North replied. "You might possibly have saved a trick."

Replay of 3

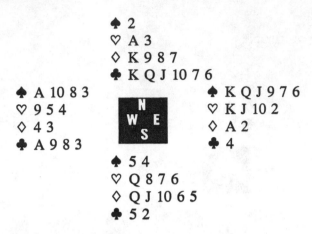

```
            ♠ 2
            ♡ A 3
            ◊ K 9 8 7
            ♣ K Q J 10 7 6
♠ A 10 8 3                    ♠ K Q J 9 7 6
♡ 9 5 4                       ♡ K J 10 2
◊ 4 3                         ◊ A 2
♣ A 9 8 3                     ♣ 4
            ♠ 5 4
            ♡ Q 8 7 6
            ◊ Q J 10 6 5
            ♣ 5 2
```

North - South sacrificed in 5 ◊ over 4 ♠. West led the ♠ A and switched to a heart. South went up with the ace and led a trump. East won and cashed the ♡ K. He then led a club and ruffed the return, for three down doubled.

South criticized his partner for going to 5 ◊ and North replied: "When you won with the ♡ A you might have tried a small stratagem that often works. Lead a high club from dummy. East plays the 4, you drop the 5, and West wins. Now there is a fair chance that West will read you for the singleton club and will lead a heart. If that happens, they lose the club ruff and you are only two down."

4 OBJECTION OVERRULED

Dealer South
North - South vulnerable

♠ 8 3
♡ A 10 2
◇ J 10 7 4
♣ K 8 5 3

◇ A led

♠ A Q 2
♡ Q 9 8 7 4
◇ K Q 9
♣ J 2

South	West	North	East
1♡	Double	2♡	Pass
Pass	2♠	Pass	Pass
3♡	Pass	Pass	Pass

West began with ace and another diamond, East playing high-low. South led a heart to the ace and played a heart back, taken by East's king. East gave his partner a diamond ruff. West exited with ace and queen of clubs and could not be prevented from taking the ♠K. This gave the defence two tricks in hearts and one in each of the other suits.

"That wasn't bad," said South. "They just about make 2♠, so we lost 100 instead of 110."

"It's better if you can make 3♡," said North thoughtfully.

"It was impossible. I had to lose five tricks after the lead."

"Sorry, I don't agree."

Replay of 4

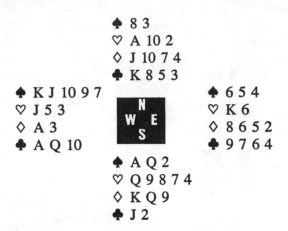

♠ 8 3
♡ A 10 2
◇ J 10 7 4
♣ K 8 5 3

♠ K J 10 9 7
♡ J 5 3
◇ A 3
♣ A Q 10

♠ 6 5 4
♡ K 6
◇ 8 6 5 2
♣ 9 7 6 4

♠ A Q 2
♡ Q 9 8 7 4
◇ K Q 9
♣ J 2

South played in 3 ♡ after West had doubled on the first round and had later bid 2 ♠. West began with ace and another diamond. South played a heart to the ace and a heart back. Now the defence took a diamond ruff. West exited with ace and queen of clubs and had only to make the ♠K, for one down.

South considered this a fair result, but North did not agree. "You want to cut down West's cards of exit," he said. "After the two rounds of diamonds lead a club. West will probably take the ace and follow with the queen. You ruff a club, then play ace and another heart. The position is:

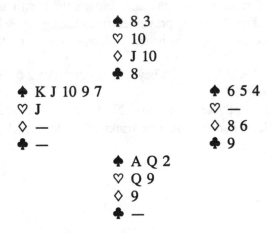

♠ 8 3
♡ 10
◇ J 10
♣ 8

♠ K J 10 9 7
♡ J
◇ —
♣ —

♠ 6 5 4
♡ —
◇ 8 6
♣ 9

♠ A Q 2
♡ Q 9
◇ 9
♣ —

"East is in. What do you want him to play? A diamond ruff doesn't help, nor does a club, which you ruff low. And if he plays a spade you go up with the ace, draw the trump, and take a discard on the fourth diamond."

5 LOSING OPTION

Dealer South
Game all

```
                    ♠ 10 2
                    ♡ A 9 7 6
                    ◇ J 10 7
                    ♣ K J 9 6

    ♠ 6 led            N
                    W     E
                       S

                    ♠ A 5 4 3
                    ♡ K Q 10 8
                    ◇ K 2
                    ♣ A 7 2
```

South	West	North	East
1 NT	Pass	2♣	2♠
3♡	Pass	4♡	Pass
Pass	Pass		

West led the ♠6, presumably a singleton. South won, drew trumps in three rounds, then finessed the ◇J. West won with the queen and led a club, which ran to the 10 and ace. When he came in with the ◇A, on which East showed out, West led a second club. South went up with the ♣K, discarded a club on the ◇10, and ruffed a club. He found the clubs 4-2, East holding Q 10 8 5, and now there was only one trump in dummy for the third and fourth spades. He found himself one down, having lost two diamonds and two spades.

"That was a shock, finding West with seven diamonds to the A Q," South remarked. "The clubs were all wrong, too."

"You didn't keep track of what was happening," said North.

"Win with the ♣K and discard a club on the ◊ 10, as you did. East has to throw a spade on this trick and now you exit with a spade. East is left on play with no safe exit. A spade lead establishes South's last spade and a club lead establishes the ♣J."

Replay of 5

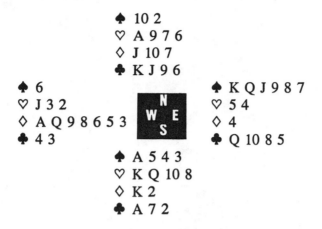

```
              ♠ 10 2
              ♡ A 9 7 6
              ◊ J 10 7
              ♣ K J 9 6
♠ 6                            ♠ K Q J 9 8 7
♡ J 3 2           N            ♡ 5 4
◊ A Q 9 8 6 5 3  W   E         ◊ 4
♣ 4 3                S         ♣ Q 10 8 5
              ♠ A 5 4 3
              ♡ K Q 10 8
              ◊ K 2
              ♣ A 7 2
```

South played in 4♡ after East had overcalled in spades. South won the spade lead, drew trumps, and ran the ◊ J to the queen. West led a club to the 10 and ace, and when he came in with the ◊ A he led another club. South went up with the king, discarded a club on the ◊ 10, and ruffed a club. There was only one trump in dummy for two spade losers, so he finished one down.

"You could count the East hand," said North. "This was the position when West led the second club:

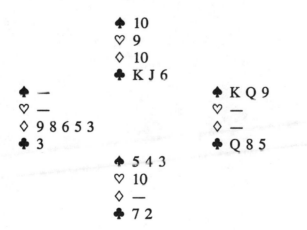

```
              ♠ 10
              ♡ 9
              ◊ 10
              ♣ K J 6
♠ —                            ♠ K Q 9
♡ —                            ♡ —
◊ 9 8 6 5 3                    ◊ —
♣ 3                            ♣ Q 8 5
              ♠ 5 4 3
              ♡ 10
              ◊ —
              ♣ 7 2
```

6 ALWAYS TIME

Dealer West
Neither side vulnerable

```
              ♠ J 4
              ♡ A Q 3
              ◊ K 7
              ♣ A J 8 7 5 3

♠ K led     ┌─────────┐
            │    N    │
            │  W   E  │
            │    S    │
            └─────────┘

              ♠ A 9 6
              ♡ 9 7 6 5
              ◊ Q 8 4
              ♣ K Q 9
```

South	West	North	East
	1 ♠	2 ♣	Pass
2 NT	Pass	3 NT	Pass
Pass	Pass		

West led the ♠ K and continued the suit; East turned up with three small. On the second round of clubs West showed out, discarding a heart. As he would not have the lead again for a heart finesse, and had only eight tricks on top, South finessed the ♡ Q. Tragedy! East won with what turned out to be a singleton king and led a diamond. The defence took six tricks — four spades, a diamond and a heart.

North sighed deeply and rested his head on his hands.

"I had to finesse while the lead was in my own hand," said South angrily. "Or perhaps you think I ought to have dropped the singleton ♡ K?"

"It might have come to that," North replied. "In any case there was no hurry to finesse."

19

Replay of 6

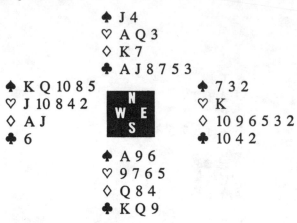

                    ♠ J 4
                    ♡ A Q 3
                    ◇ K 7
                    ♣ A J 8 7 5 3

♠ K Q 10 8 5   ♠ 7 3 2
♡ J 10 8 4 2   ♡ K
◇ A J   ◇ 10 9 6 5 3 2
♣ 6   ♣ 10 4 2

                    ♠ A 9 6
                    ♡ 9 7 6 5
                    ◇ Q 8 4
                    ♣ K Q 9

    South played in 3 NT after West had opened 1♠. Declarer won
the third round of spades, cashed two clubs, on which West discarded
a heart, then entrusted his fortunes to the heart finesse, which lost.
He finished two down.
    "I know you had no more entries to your hand," said North, "but
you could have studied the situation after a few rounds of clubs. If
West began with the guarded ♡K you would be able to finesse later.
In practice, you reach this position:

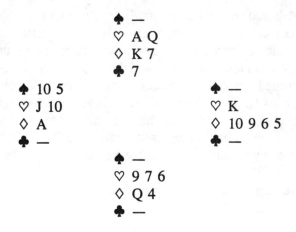

                    ♠ —
                    ♡ A Q
                    ◇ K 7
                    ♣ 7

♠ 10 5   ♠ —
♡ J 10   ♡ K
◇ A   ◇ 10 9 6 5
♣ —   ♣ —

                    ♠ —
                    ♡ 9 7 6
                    ◇ Q 4
                    ♣ —

    "What do you want West to throw on the last club? If a spade,
you can give him a diamond trick. If a fourth heart, there is a good
chance that the king will fall under the ace."

20

7 UNLUCKY DECISION

Dealer South
Both sides vulnerable

<pre>
                    ♠ 10 2
                    ♡ Q 10 8 3
                    ◇ A K 9 5
                    ♣ A 8 6

   ◇ Q led   N
                  W   E
                    S

                    ♠ A K Q 7 6
                    ♡ A K 7 6
                    ◇ 2
                    ♣ Q 9 5
</pre>

South	West	North	East
1 ♠	Pass	2 ◇	Pass
2 ♡	Pass	4 ♡	Pass
4 NT	Pass	5 ♡	Pass
6 ♡	Pass	Pass	Pass

South won the diamond lead in dummy, ruffed a diamond, and had to draw four rounds of trumps to pick up West's J 9 x x. He discarded a club on the fourth trump and a spade on the ◇ K. After cashing the three top spades, the position was then:

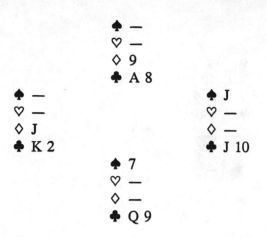

♠ —
♡ —
◇ 9
♣ A 8

♠ —
♡ —
◇ J
♣ K 2

♠ J
♡ —
◇ —
♣ J 10

♠ 7
♡ —
◇ —
♣ Q 9

South exited with a spade, on which West threw a club and dummy a diamond. East led the ♣J and South inserted the queen. "I had a count and I played the odds," he declared.

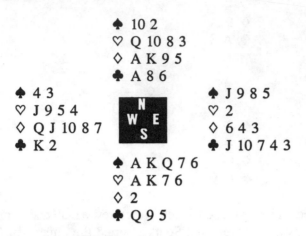

♠ 10 2
♡ Q 10 8 3
◇ A K 9 5
♣ A 8 6

♠ 4 3
♡ J 9 5 4
◇ Q J 10 8 7
♣ K 2

♠ J 9 8 5
♡ 2
◇ 6 4 3
♣ J 10 7 4 3

♠ A K Q 7 6
♡ A K 7 6
◇ 2
♣ Q 9 5

South was in 6♡ and West led the ◇ Q. South ruffed a diamond and drew trumps in four rounds, East discarding two clubs and a diamond. Declarer cashed the ◇ K and followed with the ♠ A K Q. He exited with a fourth spade, on which West had to bare the ♣ K. When East led the ♣ J at trick twelve, South went up the queen and so lost the last trick to the ♣ 10.

"I could count East for five clubs, and West for two," said South. "I think it was right to play East for the king."

"I don't disagree with that," said North. "But wasn't there a much simpler line? Ruff a diamond at trick two, as you did, and draw four rounds of trumps, discarding a club from your own hand. Then duck a spade. If the spades are not worse than 4-2 you make four tricks in spades, four top hearts, two diamonds, a diamond ruff and the ♣ A. That adds up to twelve, does it not?"

8 SPARE MAN

Dealer South
Both sides vulnerable

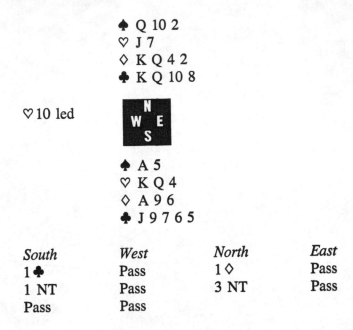

♠ Q 10 2
♡ J 7
♢ K Q 4 2
♣ K Q 10 8

♡ 10 led

♠ A 5
♡ K Q 4
♢ A 9 6
♣ J 9 7 6 5

South	West	North	East
1 ♣	Pass	1 ♢	Pass
1 NT	Pass	3 NT	Pass
Pass	Pass		

West led the ♡ 10 and South, playing in a pairs event, won with the king. On the second round of clubs East signalled in spades. West won and led a spade, covered by the 10, jack and ace. This was the position when South led the fifth club:

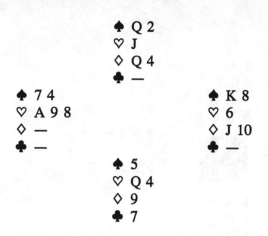

```
              ♠ Q 2
              ♡ J
              ◇ Q 4
              ♣ —
   ♠ 7 4                    ♠ K 8
   ♡ A 9 8                  ♡ 6
   ◇ —                      ◇ J 10
   ♣ —                      ♣ —
              ♠ 5
              ♡ Q 4
              ◇ 9
              ♣ 7
```

On the ♣7 dummy had no good discard. South ended with only nine tricks, a poor result.

Replay of 8

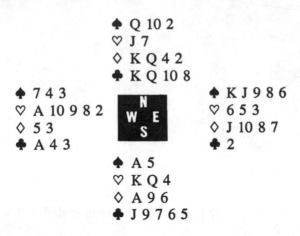

```
              ♠ Q 10 2
              ♡ J 7
              ◊ K Q 4 2
              ♣ K Q 10 8
♠ 7 4 3          N           ♠ K J 9 8 6
♡ A 10 9 8 2   W   E         ♡ 6 5 3
◊ 5 3            S           ◊ J 10 8 7
♣ A 4 3                      ♣ 2
              ♠ A 5
              ♡ K Q 4
              ◊ A 9 6
              ♣ J 9 7 6 5
```

West led the ♡10 against 3 NT. South won with the king and played on clubs. West won the second round and led a spade to the 8 and ace. When South played off his long clubs, the dummy was squeezed. South finished with only nine tricks.

"The hand contains a principle that is seldom regarded," said North pontifically. "The point is that all the cards in the North hand are busy except for the ♡7. It was essential to go up with the ♡J at trick one, retaining the 7 as a possible discard on the fifth club. This is the end position:

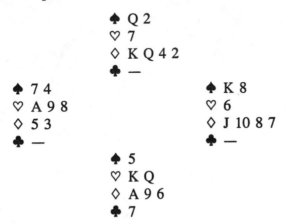

```
              ♠ Q 2
              ♡ 7
              ◊ K Q 4 2
              ♣ —
♠ 7 4            ♠ K 8
♡ A 9 8          ♡ 6
◊ 5 3            ◊ J 10 8 7
♣ —             ♣ —
              ♠ 5
              ♡ K Q
              ◊ A 9 6
              ♣ 7
```

"On the last club dummy throws a heart and it is East who has no satisfactory discard. South will make an overtrick."

9 FINESSE NOT NEEDED

Dealer North
Neither side vulnerable

$$\spadesuit \text{ A 9 6 3}$$
$$\heartsuit \text{ K J 7 6 4}$$
$$\diamondsuit \text{ 5}$$
$$\clubsuit \text{ A 10 3}$$

◊ Q led

```
    N
W       E
    S
```

$$\spadesuit \text{ K Q 8 4}$$
$$\heartsuit \text{ A 5 3}$$
$$\diamondsuit \text{ A 9 6 2}$$
$$\clubsuit \text{ J 4}$$

South	West	North	East
		1 ♡	Pass
1 ♠	Pass	2 ♠	Pass
3 ♡	Pass	4 ♣	Pass
4 ◊	Pass	5 ♠	Pass
6 ♠	Pass	Pass	Pass

South was not thinking of a slam when he bid 3 ♡ — he was simply extending a choice between the majors. However, when North showed his club control, it seemed safe to indicate the ◊ A. North's 5 ♠ was well judged. Players tend to bid 4 NT whenever a slam is in prospect; here North was not worried about aces, but about South's general strength.

West led the ◊ Q. After some thought South proceeded as follows: diamond ruff, two rounds of spades (all following), diamond ruff, heart to ace, last trump drawn, finesse of ♡ J. Unfortunately, East was able to win and produce a fourth diamond.

"I played for the best chance," South declared. "I'm all right if the heart finesse wins or if East does not hold a fourth diamond."

"If both majors are 3-2 you have twelve tricks on top," replied North.

"I don't think so. The entries are awkward."

Replay of 9

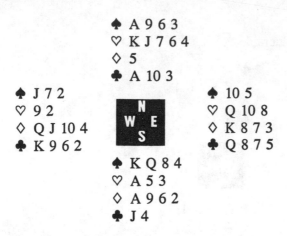

```
              ♠ A 9 6 3
              ♡ K J 7 6 4
              ◇ 5
              ♣ A 10 3
♠ J 7 2                      ♠ 10 5
♡ 9 2          N             ♡ Q 10 8
◇ Q J 10 4   W   E           ◇ K 8 7 3
♣ K 9 6 2      S             ♣ Q 8 7 5
              ♠ K Q 8 4
              ♡ A 5 3
              ◇ A 9 6 2
              ♣ J 4
```

Playing in 6♠, South won the diamond lead, ruffed a diamond, took two rounds of spades, then ruffed another diamond. He returned to the ♡A to draw the last trump, then finessed the ♡J. East won and cashed the fourth diamond.

"If the major suits are not going to break, you will have problems," North observed. "Assume, first, that they break 3-2. Now, count two diamond ruffs and four tricks in hearts. That will be enough for the slam — six trumps, four hearts and two aces."

"I played for that, as you saw," South replied. "Unfortunately, when the heart finesse lost, they had a fourth diamond to cash."

"I know. You must give up the heart trick before they can make a trick in diamonds. Win with ◇A, ruff a diamond, *now* give up a heart. What do you want them to play? It makes no difference. Say that East leads a club. You win, play ace and another spade, take a diamond ruff, back to the ♡A, and the rest is easy."

"So I give up the chance of the heart finesse?"

"Yes. You need all the entries to your own hand."

10 A DELICATE AFFAIR

Dealer South
North - South vulnerable

♠ 10 2
♡ K 8 5
◇ K J 10 8
♣ K J 7 5

♠ K led

```
    N
 W     E
    S
```

♠ Q 3
♡ A 9 7 4
◇ A Q 2
♣ A Q 8 4

South	West	North	East
1♣	1♠	Double	Pass
2♡	2♠	3♡	Pass
4♡	Pass	Pass	Pass

North had a difficult bid on the second round. He felt that a simple 3♣, following his negative double, would not express his values, so he raised the hearts, taking the view that game might be playable in a 4-3 fit.

West began with the king and ace of spades. East played high-low, evidently because he wanted his partner to play a third round of spades. West obliged, and South ruffed in dummy. He followed with three rounds of trumps, finding East with Q J x x, and so lost two trump tricks.

"I was pretty sure that the trumps would be 4-2," he said, "but there was nothing I could do about it. I don't know why you raised me with only three to the king of my second suit."

"It was because I didn't fancy 5♣, holding two losing spades and no aces. I thought there might be a play for 4♡. And so there was."

31

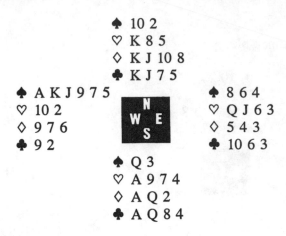

```
            ♠ 10 2
            ♡ K 8 5
            ◊ K J 10 8
            ♣ K J 7 5
♠ A K J 9 7 5                    ♠ 8 6 4
♡ 10 2           N              ♡ Q J 6 3
◊ 9 7 6        W   E            ◊ 5 4 3
♣ 9 2            S              ♣ 10 6 3
            ♠ Q 3
            ♡ A 9 7 4
            ◊ A Q 2
            ♣ A Q 8 4
```

Knowing that there was a strong spade suit against him, South played in 4♡. East played high-low on the first two spade tricks, and West co-operated by playing a third round, which was ruffed in dummy. South played king and another heart; East declined to split his honours, and South lost two trump tricks.

"It was clear that East played high-low in spades because he had at least four trumps," North pointed out. "You might have tried coming to hand with a diamond and leading a low heart to the 8 and queen. When you cash the king, West's 10 falls. Then you play off your winners in the minor suits and at trick 12 you have ♡ A 9 over East's J 6."

11 WRONG TRACK

Dealer South
Both sides vulnerable

```
              ♠ K 2
              ♡ 6 5 2
              ◊ K 10 8 7 6
              ♣ K 9 2
```

♠ 10 led

```
              ♠ A Q J
              ♡ A K 9 8 4
              ◊ 3
              ♣ 10 8 7 6
```

South	West	North	East
1 ♡	Pass	1 NT	Pass
2 ♣	Pass	3 ♡	Pass
4 ♡	Pass	Pass	Pass

South won the spade lead and played two more rounds of spades, discarding a club from dummy. He followed with a diamond, which went to the king and ace. East returned a low trump. Now, although trumps were 3-2 and the ♣A was well placed, the declarer was unable to make more than three spades, four hearts in hand, the ♣K and one club ruff.

"You gave me a lot to do there," said South. "If you bid just 2 ♡ over 2 ♣ we make a comfortable 140."

"Maybe, but I had a maximum 1 NT and a fit for your second suit — or what sounded like your second suit," North replied. "I would have been inclined to pass 1 NT on your hand. Still, as the cards lie, you might have made 4 ♡. You started off on the wrong track."

Replay of 11

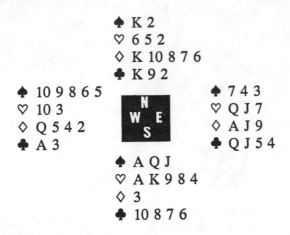

```
              ♠ K 2
              ♡ 6 5 2
              ◇ K 10 8 7 6
              ♣ K 9 2
♠ 10 9 8 6 5                    ♠ 7 4 3
♡ 10 3              N            ♡ Q J 7
◇ Q 5 4 2      W       E        ◇ A J 9
♣ A 3              S            ♣ Q J 5 4
              ♠ A Q J
              ♡ A K 9 8 4
              ◇ 3
              ♣ 10 8 7 6
```

West led the ♠10 against a borderline 4♡. South discarded a club from dummy on the third spade, then led a diamond to the king and ace. East returned a trump and, although the ♣A was right for him, South was unable to arrive at more than nine tricks.

"To begin with," said North, "I think you should lead your singleton diamond at trick two. If West has the ace it is more difficult for him, at this stage, to play low without giving some indication. Let's say that you take the right view and play low from dummy, losing to East, who will probably return a trump.

"You win with the ace, lead a spade to the king, ruff a diamond, then discard a club from dummy on the third spade. You follow with a low club. West will probably win and lead another trump. Now a club to the king and a diamond ruff, which brings down the ace. You ruff the third round of clubs and your fourth club goes away on the ◇K.

"A better defence is for West to duck when you lead a low club to the king. If this occurs, it is probably best to lead the ♣9 from dummy and hope that the clubs break 3-3.

"There was no point in playing spades early on, you see? You had to make use of all the entries to dummy to try for the option of establishing a trick with the ◇K."

12   THE STRANGLER

Dealer South
East - West vulnerable

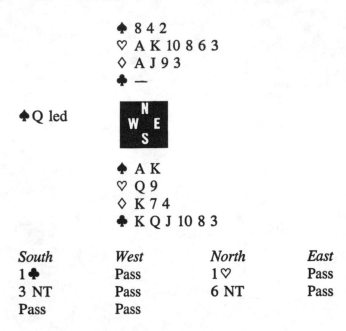

♠ 8 4 2
♡ A K 10 8 6 3
♢ A J 9 3
♣ —

♠ Q led

♠ A K
♡ Q 9
♢ K 7 4
♣ K Q J 10 8 3

South	West	North	East
1♣	Pass	1♡	Pass
3 NT	Pass	6 NT	Pass
Pass	Pass		

North's jump to 6 NT will not commend itself to scientific bidders, but at rubber bridge it was quite a sensible call. It was clear that South had a strong club suit, and if this could not be developed, either the heart or diamond suit might have provided enough tricks.

South won the spade lead and set about the clubs. The king and queen were allowed to hold, dummy discarding a spade and a heart. On a third club, won by West, the last spade was thrown from dummy and East showed out, discarding a spade. South could see:

♠ —
♡ A K 10 8 6
◇ A J 9 3
♣ —

♠ K
♡ Q 9
◇ K 7 4
♣ 10 8 3

West exited with a spade and the discard from dummy was awkward. South parted with a diamond and was a trick short when the hearts broke badly.

Replay of 12

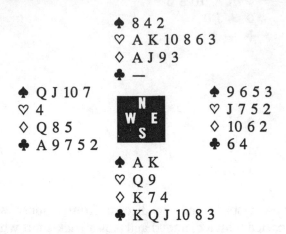

```
              ♠ 8 4 2
              ♡ A K 10 8 6 3
              ◊ A J 9 3
              ♣ —
♠ Q J 10 7              ♠ 9 6 5 3
♡ 4          N         ♡ J 7 5 2
◊ Q 8 5    W   E       ◊ 10 6 2
♣ A 9 7 5 2    S       ♣ 6 4
              ♠ A K
              ♡ Q 9
              ◊ K 7 4
              ♣ K Q J 10 8 3
```

Playing in 6 NT, South won the spade lead and played three high clubs, discarding one heart and two spades from dummy. West won the third club and exited with a spade. The declarer threw a diamond from dummy and was defeated when the hearts declined to break.

"I suppose I could have done it if I had thrown a heart from dummy instead of a diamond," said South. "I could hardly play for the diamonds to be 3-3 with the queen right."

"You strangled the dummy," his partner replied. "The third round of clubs was a mistake. First you must play a heart to the king and a heart back to the queen. Then, when you find that neither the hearts nor the clubs are breaking well, you know you have to rely on four tricks from the diamonds."

13 LOFTY ANSWER

Dealer West
Both sides vulnerable


```
            ♠ A 6 4 2
            ♡ K J 7
            ◇ A K
            ♣ 7 5 4 2
```

◇ 10 led

```
            N
        W       E
            S
```

```
            ♠ Q 3
            ♡ A Q 10 9 8 6
            ◇ Q J
            ♣ A Q 8
```

South	West	North	East
	2♣	Pass	Pass
3♡	Pass	3♠	Pass
4♣	Pass	4 NT	Pass
5♡	Pass	6♡	Pass
Pass	Pass		

North - South reached a doubtful contract after West's weak two bid, but they could point to the duplication in diamonds.

On the ◇ 10 lead East played a middle card. Trumps fell in two rounds. South cashed the second diamond, then led a low club to the 8 and West's 10. West, who began with K 10 of clubs, sensibly exited with the king and in time South lost a spade trick.

"I was playing West for any singleton in clubs," South explained. "In that case he would have had to return a spade and I wouldn't have lost any more tricks."

"That was a possibility, I suppose," said North, "but it was by no means the best plan."

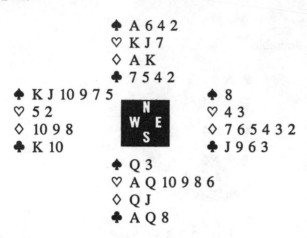

```
          ♠ A 6 4 2
          ♡ K J 7
          ◇ A K
          ♣ 7 5 4 2
♠ K J 10 9 7 5              ♠ 8
♡ 5 2                      ♡ 4 3
◇ 10 9 8                   ◇ 7 6 5 4 3 2
♣ K 10                     ♣ J 9 6 3
          ♠ Q 3
          ♡ A Q 10 9 8 6
          ◇ Q J
          ♣ A Q 8
```

North - South reached 6♡ after West had opened with a weak
2♠ bid. West led a diamond. After the trumps had fallen in two
rounds South cashed the second diamond, then ducked a club to West.
West returned the ♣K and in time South had to lose a spade trick.

"My line wins against any singleton club in the West hand," South
remarked. "Playing the ace first is no good in that case, even if a
singleton king falls."

"That is true," said North, "but there were grounds for taking
West to be 6-2-3-2 and also to hold the ♣K. I think you have more
chances if you play ace and another. You leave him on play."

"I thought of that," said South loftily. "But of course West will
drop the ♣K under the ace."

"That doesn't help him," North replied. "You play the ♣A early
on. When the king is played you cross to dummy with the second
diamond and lead another club, intending to put in the 8. East may
prevent this by inserting the jack; then you win and return the 8,
establishing a trick for dummy's 7."

14 THE LUCK WAS THERE

Dealer South
Both sides vulnerable

♠ A 8 5
♡ 8 6 4 2
◇ J 5 3
♣ Q 10 4

◇ K led

```
    N
  W   E
    S
```

♠ K Q J 10 9 6 2
♡ A 9 3
◇ —
♣ K 7 5

South	West	North	East
1 ♠	Pass	1 NT	Pass
4 ♠	Pass	Pass	Pass

South ruffed the diamond lead, drew trumps in two rounds, then played ace and another heart, on which West played the 10 and queen, East the 5 and 7. West led another diamond and South ruffed. West discarded on the third round of hearts and in the end South lost two club tricks, to finish one down.

"All I wanted was a bit of luck in either hearts or clubs," South remarked.

"The luck was there if you had known where to look for it," North replied.

Replay of **14**

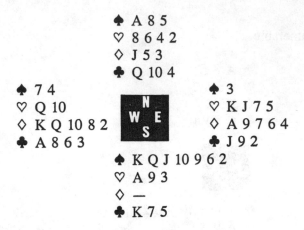

```
                    ♠ A 8 5
                    ♡ 8 6 4 2
                    ◇ J 5 3
                    ♣ Q 10 4
  ♠ 7 4                           ♠ 3
  ♡ Q 10          N              ♡ K J 7 5
  ◇ K Q 10 8 2  W   E            ◇ A 9 7 6 4
  ♣ A 8 6 3       S              ♣ J 9 2
                    ♠ K Q J 10 9 6 2
                    ♡ A 9 3
                    ◇ —
                    ♣ K 7 5
```

Playing in 4 ♠ , South ruffed the diamond lead, drew trumps, then played ace and another heart. He ruffed the second round of diamonds and played a third heart. After ruffing the fourth round of hearts he lost to the jack and ace of clubs.

"It must be right in general to eliminate the diamonds," North pointed out. "Cross to dummy with a trump, ruff the second diamond, then cross to the ♠ 8 and ruff the last diamond. At this point lead ace and another heart. East cannot afford to overtake, so the position is:

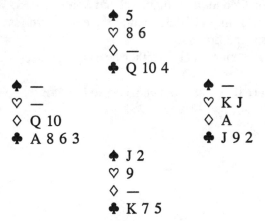

```
                    ♠ 5
                    ♡ 8 6
                    ◇ —
                    ♣ Q 10 4
  ♠ —                           ♠ —
  ♡ —                           ♡ K J
  ◇ Q 10                        ◇ A
  ♣ A 8 6 3                     ♣ J 9 2
                    ♠ J 2
                    ♡ 9
                    ◇ —
                    ♣ K 7 5
```

"West has to open up the clubs. The 10 is covered by the jack and king, and you make a second trick with the queen."

15   NOT A GUESS

Dealer North
Neither side vulnerable

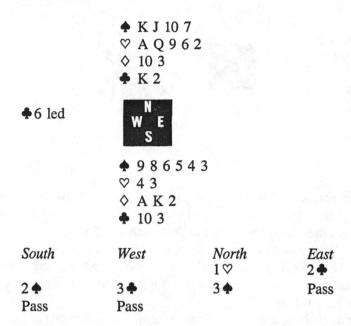

♠ K J 10 7
♡ A Q 9 6 2
♦ 10 3
♣ K 2

♣6 led

♠ 9 8 6 5 4 3
♡ 4 3
♦ A K 2
♣ 10 3

South	West	North	East
		1♡	2♣
2♠	3♣	3♠	Pass
Pass	Pass		

In these days of negative doubles a response at the two level in a higher valued suit, South's 2♠ bid on this occasion, is generally played as non-forcing.

The defence won the first two tricks in clubs, then East exited with a low diamond. South led a spade and went into a trance when West played low. Eventually he ran the 9, losing to the singleton queen. As the heart finesse was wrong too, South finished one down, losing two spades, two clubs and a heart.

"It was a pure guess," said the declarer.

"Not a guess at all," replied his partner with some asperity.

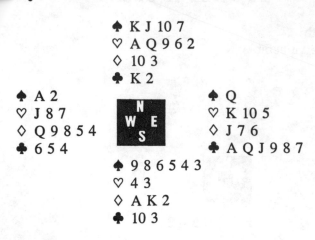

```
              ♠ K J 10 7
              ♡ A Q 9 6 2
              ◇ 10 3
              ♣ K 2
♠ A 2                        ♠ Q
♡ J 8 7          N          ♡ K 10 5
◇ Q 9 8 5 4   W   E        ◇ J 7 6
♣ 6 5 4          S          ♣ A Q J 9 8 7
              ♠ 9 8 6 5 4 3
              ♡ 4 3
              ◇ A K 2
              ♣ 10 3
```

South played in 3♠ after East had overcalled 2♣ and West had raised. The defence took two tricks in clubs and exited with a diamond. South lost a spade finesse to the queen and finished one down.

"The hand was an example of what the textbooks call 'Assumption'," North declared. "If the heart finesse is right you can't lose the contract, so you assume it will be wrong. In that case West is sure to hold the ♠A."

"He might have had A Q x," said South. "I was thinking of that."

"Not likely, because with a void in spades, the ♡K and six clubs to the A Q J East would probably have gone to 4♣. Incidentally, if you had been in 4♠ you would have had to assume that West held the ♡K and therefore East the ♠A."

16   COLLAPSE OF STOUT PARTY

Dealer South
East - West vulnerable

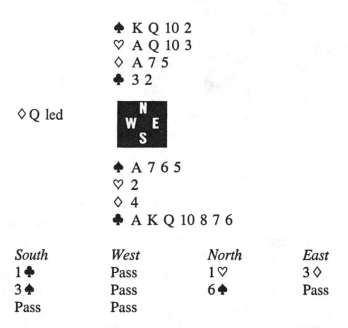

♠ K Q 10 2
♡ A Q 10 3
◊ A 7 5
♣ 3 2

◊ Q led

♠ A 7 6 5
♡ 2
◊ 4
♣ A K Q 10 8 7 6

South	West	North	East
1♣	Pass	1♡	3◊
3♠	Pass	6♠	Pass
Pass	Pass		

South's 3♠ bid was not well judged, as these top-heavy hands seldom play well except in the long suit. On this occasion, however, North had excellent support for spades.

South won the diamond lead in dummy, played the ♠K and a spade to the ace. East showed out on the second round of trumps. Declarer drew the outstanding spades, then led a club, but East showed out again. The contract now went several down.

"I could have saved a trick or two by leading a club earlier and playing on cross-ruff lines," South admitted.

"You could have done better than that," his partner replied. "The contract was lay-down."

Replay of 16

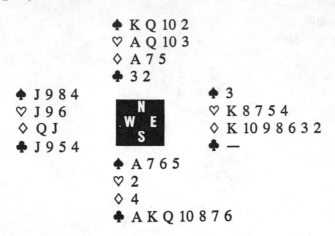

                    ♠ K Q 10 2
                    ♡ A Q 10 3
                    ◊ A 7 5
                    ♣ 3 2

    ♠ J 9 8 4   ♠ 3
    ♡ J 9 6   ♡ K 8 7 5 4
    ◊ Q J   ◊ K 10 9 8 6 3 2
    ♣ J 9 5 4   ♣ —

                    ♠ A 7 6 5
                    ♡ 2
                    ◊ 4
                    ♣ A K Q 10 8 7 6

South played in 6♣ after East had made a jump bid in diamonds.
He won the diamond lead in dummy, played the ♠K and a spade
to the ace, and drew all the trumps. The contract collapsed when
the clubs turned out to be 4-0.

While it is normally correct with this trump combination to play
king first and low to the ace, on this occasion South must be careful
not to take away entries to his own hand. The safe play is king and
queen of spades from dummy. When East shows out, South plays
a club to the ace, ruffs the third round, and plays a trump to the ace.
All he loses is one trump trick.

17 MEDAL CHANCE

Dealer South
Neither side vulnerable

```
                    ♠ Q 7 4
                    ♡ A K Q J 10 9
                    ◊ A J
                    ♣ 7 2

  ♠ 10 led        N
                W   E
                    S

                    ♠ A J 6
                    ♡ 3
                    ◊ K 10
                    ♣ A K 10 9 8 6 5
```

South	West	North	East
1♣	Pass	2♡	Pass
3♣	Pass	4♡	Pass
4 NT	Pass	5♡	Pass
7 NT	Pass	Pass	Pass

South's 7 NT was a reasonable venture in a pairs event. North had shown solid hearts by the jump to 4♡, and if there was a loser in the club suit there would surely be other chances.

West's lead of the ♠ 10 ran to the jack. South played off six hearts, followed by two diamonds and the ♠ A. Since West held three clubs and East ♠ K x x, neither defender was embarrassed.

"Next time I'll let you play this type of hand in 7♡," said the declarer sadly. "Mind you, we only wanted a club break or the ♠ K in the same hand as the long clubs."

"You didn't give yourself the best chance," said North bleakly.

Replay of 17

```
              ♠ Q 7 4
              ♡ A K Q J 10 9
              ◊ A J
              ♣ 7 2
♠ 10 9 8 5              ♠ K 3 2
♡ 8 7 6       N        ♡ 5 4 2
◊ 9 4 2     W   E      ◊ Q 8 7 6 5 3
♣ J 4 3       S        ♣ Q
              ♠ A J 6
              ♡ 3
              ◊ K 10
              ♣ A K 10 9 8 6 5
```

South played in 7 NT and West led the ♠10, which ran to the jack. With the general idea of squeezing East in spades and clubs, South played off six hearts, the ♠A and two diamonds. East was able to keep the ♠K and West the guard in clubs.

"It would have been a good idea to lay down the ♣A early on," said North. "As it happens, East has to drop the queen. That's not a likely card from Q J x, so it will look as though clubs are 2-2 or that West has three. After the ♣A cross to dummy with a heart and lead the ♠Q to transfer the menace. Run off all the red winners and you will have a simple squeeze."

"Suppose East doesn't cover the ♠Q?"

"You can give him a medal; but you should let the queen run because players don't often lead from a king against 7 NT."

18 DISAPPEARING TRICK

Dealer West
East - West vulnerable

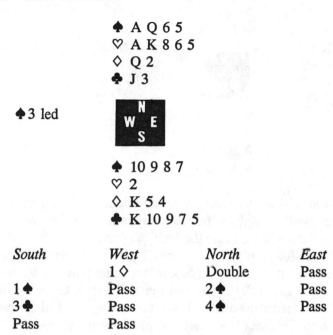

♠ A Q 6 5
♡ A K 8 6 5
◇ Q 2
♣ J 3

♠3 led

♠ 10 9 8 7
♡ 2
◇ K 5 4
♣ K 10 9 7 5

South	West	North	East
	1 ◇	Double	Pass
1 ♠	Pass	2 ♠	Pass
3 ♣	Pass	4 ♠	Pass
Pass	Pass		

West led a low trump and South played low from dummy. East won with the jack and returned a club. That was the end of the story, as West held the ♣ A Q and the ◇ A.

"I dare say I ought to have gone in with the ♠Q on the first trick," South remarked, "but there are still four top losers — a trump, a diamond, and two clubs."

"It may look like that," his partner replied, "but I can see other possibilities."

Replay of 18

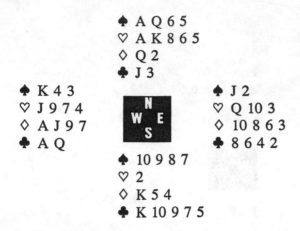

♠ A Q 6 5
♡ A K 8 6 5
◇ Q 2
♣ J 3

♠ K 4 3
♡ J 9 7 4
◇ A J 9 7
♣ A Q

♠ J 2
♡ Q 10 3
◇ 10 8 6 3
♣ 8 6 4 2

♠ 10 9 8 7
♡ 2
◇ K 5 4
♣ K 10 9 7 5

South was in 4♠ and West, who had opened the bidding, led a low trump. South played low from dummy, and when East won with the jack and returned a club, the hand was over.

"There are four top losers however I play it," South declared.

"I wonder," said North. "You can put some pressure on West. Suppose you win the first trick with the ♠Q, come to hand with a heart ruff, and lead a low diamond. West must play low and the queen wins. You ruff another low heart and play a spade to the ace. The position is then:

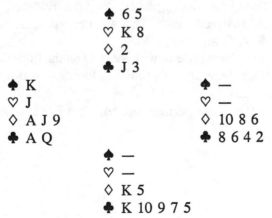

♠ 6 5
♡ K 8
◇ 2
♣ J 3

♠ K
♡ J
◇ A J 9
♣ A Q

♠ —
♡ —
◇ 10 8 6
♣ 8 6 4 2

♠ —
♡ —
◇ K 5
♣ K 10 9 7 5

"You cash the ♡K and exit with a trump. West can make his two aces, but that's all."

19 TWO-TWO TO TOOTING

Dealer South
Both sides vulnerable

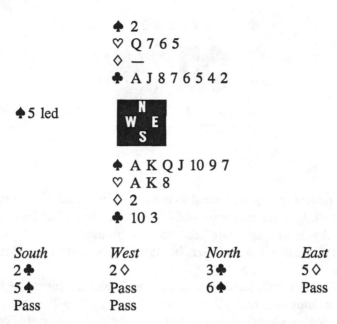

♠ 2
♡ Q 7 6 5
◇ —
♣ A J 8 7 6 5 4 2

♠ 5 led

♠ A K Q J 10 9 7
♡ A K 8
◇ 2
♣ 10 3

South	West	North	East
2♣	2◇	3♣	5◇
5♠	Pass	6♠	Pass
Pass	Pass		

6♣ would have been a safe contract as the cards lay, but from North's angle his partner might have held a low singleton. Meanwhile, he had fair support for the spades, which were almost sure to be solid.

West found the excellent lead of a trump. South played off all his spades and tried to find the extra trick in hearts, but the defence was not tested. East kept his guard in hearts and two clubs.

"The trump lead was fatal," said South. "Apart from stopping the diamond ruff it left me with two losers and bad timing for a squeeze. If I duck a club, they cash a diamond."

"It was a question of the two-two to Tooting," said North cryptically.

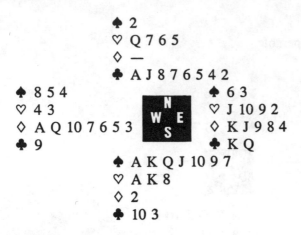

```
              ♠ 2
              ♡ Q 7 6 5
              ◊ —
              ♣ A J 8 7 6 5 4 2
♠ 8 5 4                        ♠ 6 3
♡ 4 3             N            ♡ J 10 9 2
◊ A Q 10 7 6 5 3  W   E        ◊ K J 9 8 4
♣ 9               S            ♣ K Q
              ♠ A K Q J 10 9 7
              ♡ A K 8
              ◊ 2
              ♣ 10 3
```

South played in 6♠ and West found the killing lead of a trump. At least, it killed South. He played off all his spades, but East had no difficulty in keeping four hearts and two clubs.

"I can play off the ♣A earlier, but it makes no difference," said the declarer.

"You had to rectify the count, as they say," North replied. "After drawing trumps lead the ◊2 and discard dummy's ♣2. Later you play the ♣A, a simple Vienna coup, and the timing is right for a squeeze against East."

20 BACKSTAGE

Dealer North
Both sides vulnerable

        ♠ K J 8
        ♡ 2
        ◇ K Q 10 8 7 6 5
        ♣ K Q

♡9 led

        N
      W   E
        S

        ♠ A 10 9 7 6 5
        ♡ 10 3
        ◇ J 4 3
        ♣ A 2

South	West	North	East
		1 ◇	2 ♡
2 ♣	4 ♡	4 ♠	5 ♡
5 ♠	Pass	Pass	Pass

South's 5♠ certainly doesn't look right. He should have let 5♡ run to his partner, and North would have doubled.

West led the ♡9 against 5♠ and East returned the ♣J. South won in hand, ruffed a heart with the ♣J, then played the ♠K and a spade to the ace. West showed out, so the contract was one down.

"I knew the trumps were likely to be 3-1," South remarked, "but it wasn't convenient to finesse through West, and East wasn't likely to have the length."

"You might have changed your mind when East followed to the second spade," North replied. "As you say, the trumps were more likely to be 3-1 than 2-2. Apart from that, there was a sound reason to play East for the trump length."

Replay of 20

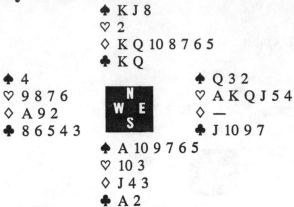

♠ K J 8
♥ 2
♦ K Q 10 8 7 6 5
♣ K Q

♠ 4
♥ 9 8 7 6
♦ A 9 2
♣ 8 6 5 4 3

♠ Q 3 2
♥ A K Q J 5 4
♦ —
♣ J 10 9 7

♠ A 10 9 7 6 5
♥ 10 3
♦ J 4 3
♣ A 2

South played in 5♠ after East - West had bid to 5♥. West led a heart and East shifted to the ♣J. South won, ruffed his second heart with the ♠J, then played ♠K and a spade to the ace. Now he had to go one down.

"I agree," said North, "that initially West was more likely to hold three trumps than East, who was marked with at least six hearts. However, it is sometimes advisable to look behind the scenes. What is the diamond situation? If West had held a low singleton he would have led it, and if East had held a singleton he would have returned it. A singleton ace was possible, admittedly, but on balance the most likely explanation was that West held A x x. This changes the odds, and since a 2-2 break in trumps was unlikely, you should have finessed against East when he followed to the second round."

21 BLIND ALLEY

Dealer South
East - West vulnerable

```
            ♠ A 9 8 6 2
            ♡ 6 5
            ◇ A K J 9 4
            ♣ 5
♠K led      ┌─────────┐
            │   N     │
            │ W   E   │
            │   S     │
            └─────────┘
            ♠ 4
            ♡ A K Q J 10 8
            ◇ 3
            ♣ A Q J 7 3
```

South	West	North	East
2♡	Pass	2♠	Pass
3♣	Pass	3◇	Pass
4♡	Pass	6♡	Pass
Pass	Pass		

South opened with an Acol two bid and his jump to 4♡ was intended to give an accurate picture of his hand — solid hearts with a fair side suit.

West led a spade to dummy's ace and South's line was to play the ♣A and run the queen, which held the trick. However, the next club was ruffed and overruffed. East returned a trump and at the finish South, who had eleven tricks on top, tried vainly for a squeeze.

"What do you think of that?" South exclaimed. "The clubs had to be 5-2, East had to return a trump after overruffing, and the diamond finesse had to be wrong, with no chance of a squeeze."

"Just don't ask me what I thought of it," North replied. "Twelve tricks were cold."

Replay of 21

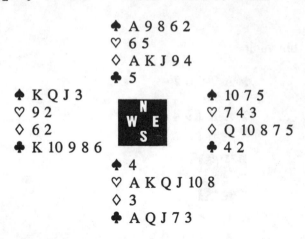

♠ A 9 8 6 2
♡ 6 5
♢ A K J 9 4
♣ 5

♠ K Q J 3
♡ 9 2
♢ 6 2
♣ K 10 9 8 6

♠ 10 7 5
♡ 7 4 3
♢ Q 10 8 7 5
♣ 4 2

♠ 4
♡ A K Q J 10 8
♢ 3
♣ A Q J 7 3

South played in 6♡. West should have led a trump — not that it would have made any difference. In practice he began with the ♠K, which was won in the dummy. South played a club to the ace and returned the queen, which West correctly declined to cover. Then a low club was overruffed by East and a trump was returned. South had eleven tricks on top but was unable to develop a twelfth.

"You had some sort of blind spot," North observed. "Don't play ♣A and then the queen. Simply ruff a low club and then draw trumps. Your ♣Q J are equals against the king and the fifth club goes away on the ♢K."

Dealer South
Both sides vulnerable

```
              ♠ Q 9 7 6 5
              ♡ K
              ◇ A 8 6 4 3
              ♣ A 2

♠ A led           N
                W   E
                  S

              ♠ 4 2
              ♡ A 10 8 7 6 5 4
              ◇ Q 10 9
              ♣ K
```

South	West	North	East
3♡	Pass	Pass	Pass

Not every player would fancy a 3♡ opening on the South hand — but this one did.

West began with ace and another spade. East won with the jack and returned the ♡Q. South came to hand with a club and cashed the ♡A. As the trumps were 4-1 he had to lose two more hearts and a diamond, for one down.

"That may not be a good result," remarked South, who was playing in a pairs. "There's nothing on for them."

"It certainly won't be a good result," replied his partner. "It seemed to me that you didn't try very hard to make it."

Replay of 22

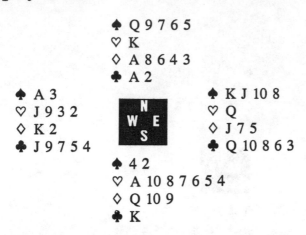

```
              ♠ Q 9 7 6 5
              ♡ K
              ◇ A 8 6 4 3
              ♣ A 2
♠ A 3                          ♠ K J 10 8
♡ J 9 3 2         N            ♡ Q
◇ K 2          W     E         ◇ J 7 5
♣ J 9 7 5 4       S            ♣ Q 10 8 6 3
              ♠ 4 2
              ♡ A 10 8 7 6 5 4
              ◇ Q 10 9
              ♣ K
```

South opened 3♡ and there was no competition. West led the ♠A and followed with a spade to the jack. East returned the ♡Q. South crossed to the ♣K and played off the ♡A. He ended one down, having lost two spades, two hearts and a diamond.

"You must try to do something with the fifth spade," said North. "When you win with the ♡K lead a third spade and ruff low. It is evident from the way the play has gone that West has the length in hearts. Say that West overruffs and exits with a club. You win with the king and play ace and another heart. What can West do now? If he plays another club you win in dummy and ruff the fourth round of spades, with the ◇A as an entry for the fifth spade."

23   JUST AN IDEA

Dealer East
East - West vulnerable

♢ 4 led

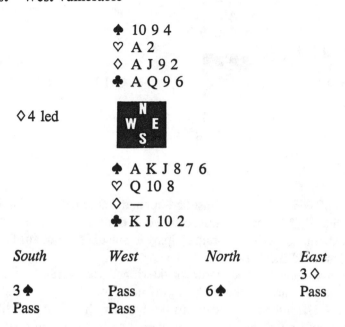

$\spadesuit$ 10 9 4
$\heartsuit$ A 2
$\diamondsuit$ A J 9 2
$\clubsuit$ A Q 9 6

$\spadesuit$ A K J 8 7 6
$\heartsuit$ Q 10 8
$\diamondsuit$ —
$\clubsuit$ K J 10 2

South	West	North	East
			3 ♢
3 ♠	Pass	6 ♠	Pass
Pass	Pass		

North's jump to six was not just a blunderbuss: it expressed the values and conveyed the inference that all the top controls were held.

However, the hands did not fit too well. South went up with the ♢ A, discarding a heart, and played the ace and king of spades, finding West with the expected Q x x. He then played for an elimination ending: club to dummy, diamond ruff, and three more rounds of clubs. West ruffed the fourth round and led a heart; East held the king and South was one down.

"I played for the only chance," South declared. "I had to find West with the ♡ K."

"That wasn't likely," said North. "Would East open 3 ♢, vulnerable, with nothing but seven to the K Q 10? Some players do that sort of thing, but not our illustrious opponent. There was another way to play the hand; not guaranteed, but it might have worked."

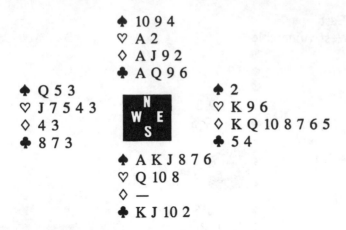

```
            ♠ 10 9 4
            ♡ A 2
            ◇ A J 9 2
            ♣ A Q 9 6
♠ Q 5 3                      ♠ 2
♡ J 7 5 4 3                  ♡ K 9 6
◇ 4 3                        ◇ K Q 10 8 7 6 5
♣ 8 7 3                      ♣ 5 4
            ♠ A K J 8 7 6
            ♡ Q 10 8
            ◇ —
            ♣ K J 10 2
```

South played in 6♠ after East had opened 3◇. Declarer won the diamond lead, drew two trumps, crossed to dummy with a club, and ruffed a diamond. He tried for an endplay against West, but this failed since East held the ♡K.

"There was another line worth considering," said North. "Discard a club, not a heart, on the ◇A, then finesse on the first round of trumps. West, after all, is likely to hold Q x x. It is quite possible that West will return a diamond, or even a club. Then you play for this ending:

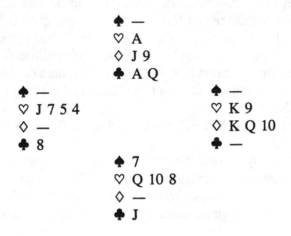

```
            ♠ —
            ♡ A
            ◇ J 9
            ♣ A Q
♠ —                          ♠ —
♡ J 7 5 4                    ♡ K 9
◇ —                          ◇ K Q 10
♣ 8                          ♣ —
            ♠ 7
            ♡ Q 10 8
            ◇ —
            ♣ J
```

"A club is led to dummy and East is squeezed on the last club."

"You'd look silly if trumps were 2-2 and West switched to a heart when he was in the with ♠Q."

"I know, but it's important to finesse on the first round of trumps, before East can signal."

24 A SLIGHT DIFFERENCE

Dealer West
North - South vulnerable

```
              ♠ Q 5 4
              ♡ 8 6 2
              ◇ K Q 3
              ♣ 8 4 3 2
♡5 led           N
              W     E
                 S
              ♠ K 9 7 6 2
              ♡ A K 4
              ◇ A 7 5
              ♣ K Q
```

South	West	North	East
	Pass	Pass	1♡
Double	Pass	2♣	Pass
2♠	Pass	3♠	Pass
4♠	Double	Pass	Pass
Pass			

West led the ♡5 and East played the 9. South won, crossed to dummy with a diamond, and led a low spade, which ran to the 3, king and ace. West led a second heart and, as the trumps were 4-1, South lost three spades, a heart and a club.

"I led the low spade from dummy," South explained, "because if East turned up with 8, 10 or jack I would be able to hold West to two tricks in the suit. You didn't have much for your raise to 3♠, did you?"

"I had enough," North replied. "Enough for you to make 4♠, anyway."

Replay of 24

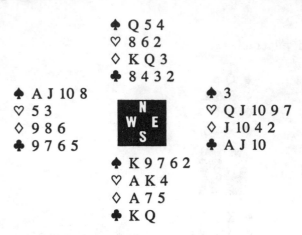

```
              ♠ Q 5 4
              ♡ 8 6 2
              ◇ K Q 3
              ♣ 8 4 3 2
♠ A J 10 8                    ♠ 3
♡ 5 3           N            ♡ Q J 10 9 7
◇ 9 8 6       W   E          ◇ J 10 4 2
♣ 9 7 6 5       S            ♣ A J 10
              ♠ K 9 7 6 2
              ♡ A K 4
              ◇ A 7 5
              ♣ K Q
```

South played in 4♠ doubled after East had opened third in hand.
Declarer won the heart lead, played a diamond to dummy and led
a low spade to the king. West won and led his second heart. Now
South had to go two down, losing three spades, a heart and a club.

"You didn't pay enough attention to the double," said North.
"After the heart lead you should knock out the ♣A, to kill the East
hand if he has the ace. You win the second heart and eliminate the
diamonds and clubs, ruffing twice. This is the ending:

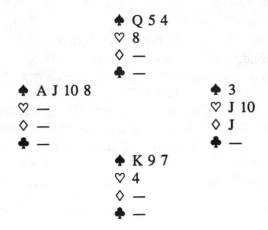

```
              ♠ Q 5 4
              ♡ 8
              ◇ —
              ♣ —
♠ A J 10 8                    ♠ 3
♡ —                          ♡ J 10
◇ —                          ◇ J
♣ —                          ♣ —
              ♠ K 9 7
              ♡ 4
              ◇ —
              ♣ —
```

"Now you lead a heart; West has to ruff his partner's trick and
lose one of his spade tricks as well."

25 OTHER WAY UP

Dealer West
Both sides vulnerable

<pre>
                    ♠ J 7 5 2
                    ♡ 2
                    ◇ K 10 8 7
                    ♣ A 9 7 5
                         N
  ♡ Q led   W   E
                         S
                    ♠ K 6 3
                    ♡ A K 5 4
                    ◇ A Q J 9 6
                    ♣ 2
</pre>

South	West	North	East
South	*West*	*North*	*East*
	1 ♡	Pass	Pass
Double	Pass	1 ♠	Pass
2 ◇	Pass	4 ◇	Pass
5 ◇	Pass	Pass	Pass

South won the heart lead, ruffed a heart, returned to hand with a trump, and ruffed another heart. After drawing trumps he led a low spade from hand, hoping to find West with A x or A Q. But the spades were 3-3, West holding A x x, and South went one down, losing three spade tricks.

The declarer was confident that he had played for the best chance. His partner did not agree.

Replay of 25

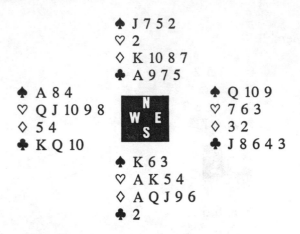

```
            ♠ J 7 5 2
            ♡ 2
            ◇ K 10 8 7
            ♣ A 9 7 5
♠ A 8 4                      ♠ Q 10 9
♡ Q J 10 9 8    N            ♡ 7 6 3
◇ 5 4          W   E         ◇ 3 2
♣ K Q 10        S            ♣ J 8 6 4 3
            ♠ K 6 3
            ♡ A K 5 4
            ◇ A Q J 9 6
            ♣ 2
```

West, who had opened the bidding with 1 ♡, led the ♡Q against South's 5 ◇. South took two heart ruffs but had to lose three spade tricks at the finish, or the equivalent.

"I can do it if West has any doubleton in spades," South remarked.

"I don't think you played the right game here," North replied. "Instead of ruffing two hearts in dummy, why not ruff three clubs in hand? You make the same number of trump tricks and put West under more pressure. This is the end-game:

```
            ♠ J 7 5 2
            ♡ —
            ◇ K
            ♣ —
♠ A 8 4                      ♠ Q 10 9
♡ J 10                       ♡ —
◇ —                          ◇ —
♣ —                          ♣ J 8
            ♠ K 6 3
            ♡ K 5
            ◇ —
            ♣ —
```

"Now you just play king and another heart, leaving West on play. If West keeps two spades and three hearts, then of course you play a spade from hand in the diagram position."

26 DON'T STOP!

Dealer West
East - West vulnerable

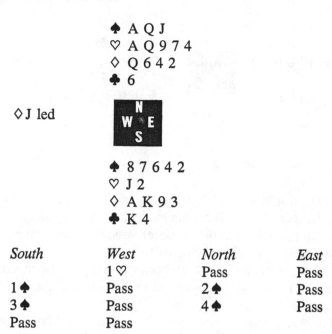

♠ A Q J
♡ A Q 9 7 4
◊ Q 6 4 2
♣ 6

◊ J led

♠ 8 7 6 4 2
♡ J 2
◊ A K 9 3
♣ K 4

South	West	North	East
	1 ♡	Pass	Pass
1 ♠	Pass	2 ♠	Pass
3 ♠	Pass	4 ♠	Pass
Pass	Pass		

The ◊ J ran to South's king and a finesse of the ♠ Q held. South attempted to come back to hand with a diamond, but West ruffed with the ♠ K and led a heart, which his partner ruffed. West came in again with the ♣ A, and a second heart ruff followed. One down!

"That was the most remarkable feat I have ever seen," said North, as he entered 50 to the opposition.

"What do you mean? I know I could have made it if I had drawn the ♠ A, but I didn't know the king was going to fall. I suppose I could have made eleven tricks, actually."

"Don't stop."

"What? Oh, I suppose I can make three tricks in hearts as the cards lie. That's twelve in all."

"Don't stop."

Replay of 26

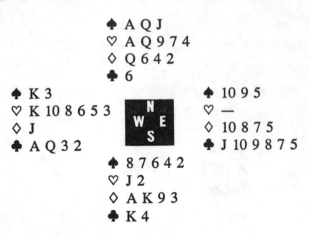

```
              ♠ A Q J
              ♡ A Q 9 7 4
              ◇ Q 6 4 2
              ♣ 6
♠ K 3                         ♠ 10 9 5
♡ K 10 8 6 5 3      N         ♡ —
◇ J             W       E     ◇ 10 8 7 5
♣ A Q 3 2           S         ♣ J 10 9 8 7 5
              ♠ 8 7 6 4 2
              ♡ J 2
              ◇ A K 9 3
              ♣ K 4
```

South played in 4♠ after West had opened 1♡. The ◇J ran to the ace and a spade finesse held. South unwisely attempted to regain the lead with the ◇K, and then disaster struck in the form of diamond ruff, heart ruff, ♣A, heart ruff.

South admitted that it would have been wiser to play the ♠A after the queen had held. Even if West had held K 10 9 x, the contract would have been safe.

With the ♠K falling under the ace, there would have been twelve tricks by way of five spades, four diamonds and three hearts. As South, at the finish, holds ♣ K x, a low heart, and a trump, while dummy has ♡Q 9 7, the last trump squeezes West, who has to find a discard from ♡10 8 6 and the ♣A.

27 ON THE RIGHT SIDE

Dealer West
North - South vulnerable

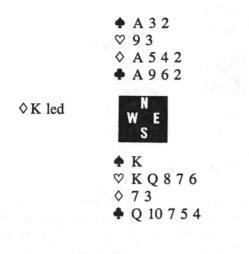

♠ A 3 2
♡ 9 3
◊ A 5 4 2
♣ A 9 6 2

◊ K led

♠ K
♡ K Q 8 7 6
◊ 7 3
♣ Q 10 7 5 4

South	West	North	East
	1 ♡	Double	1 ♠
2 ♣	2 ♠	3 ♣	3 ♠
5 ♣	Pass	Pass	Pass

North's 3♣ was on the forward side; South's jump to 5♣ was reasonable after his cautious 2♣.

Declarer won the diamond lead, crossed to the ♠K, and returned to the ♣A to discard his diamond on the ♠A. West was 3-5-3-2 and at this point the contract could not be made. If South plays hearts he will run into a ruff, and if he plays a second round of trumps he will not have enough entries to set up his fifth heart.

"You didn't have a lot for your raise," South remarked. "I think my only hope was to find West with a singleton ♣K."

"That was a possibility, I suppose," North replied. "But East played a high diamond on the first trick and was likely to be 6-1-4-2. I think you set about it the wrong way."

Replay of 27

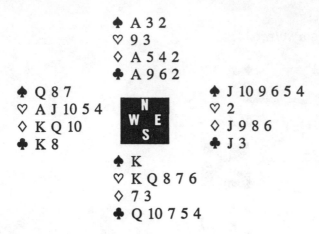

```
              ♠ A 3 2
              ♡ 9 3
              ◇ A 5 4 2
              ♣ A 9 6 2
♠ Q 8 7                      ♠ J 10 9 6 5 4
♡ A J 10 5 4                 ♡ 2
◇ K Q 10                     ◇ J 9 8 6
♣ K 8                        ♣ J 3
              ♠ K
              ♡ K Q 8 7 6
              ◇ 7 3
              ♣ Q 10 7 5 4
```

South was in 5♣ and West led the ◇K. South took the ace in dummy, crossed to the ♠K, and led a club to the ace. His diamond loser went away on the ♠A but he was still a trick short. If he plays a club, for example, West will lead a diamond and South will be short of entries to establish an extra winner in hearts.

"Suppose you begin with the ♣Q instead of a low one," North suggested. "West covers, you win with the ace, discard the diamond loser, and play on hearts. Now, if West plays a club to the jack you have enough entries to get the fifth heart going. And if West plays another diamond, say, you ruff and lead another high heart. East can ruff with the jack of trumps, but you continue on crossruff lines and make the rest."

"That's very double-dummy. Why should it be better to lead the ♣Q and leave East with the jack than to lead low and leave West with the king?"

"The point is that you can't afford to draw a second round of trumps. It won't be fatal if East ruffs a heart with the master trump, so you play him for J x."

28 NO HURRY

Dealer East
North - South vulnerable

```
            ♠ K 9 3
            ♡ A 8 7
            ◇ A Q 10 2
            ♣ 9 5 3
```

◇ J led

```
        N
    W       E
        S
```

```
            ♠ A 10 7 6 5 4
            ♡ Q 10
            ◇ 3
            ♣ Q 10 8 6
```

South	West	North	East
			1 ◇
1 ♠	Pass	2 ◇	3 ♣
Pass	3 ◇	3 ♠	Pass
Pass	Pass		

North attempted to push his partner into game, but South judged correctly that with diamonds and clubs bid on his right the hand might not play well.

Declarer won the lead of the ◇ J in dummy and led a low spade to the ace, expecting to find East with a singleton. East, however, showed out, discarding a diamond. South returned a spade to the king, West splitting his honours. The ◇ Q was covered and ruffed, then West was put in with the ♣ Q. West exited with a heart. South let this run to the king — to play the ace and take a discard is worse. The defence still had to make the top clubs and a club ruff, so South was one down.

"Lucky we weren't in four," South remarked. "I was entitled to bid the game, but I could see the suits weren't going to break well."

"Yes, you did well to pass 3 ♠; but why didn't you make it?"

Replay of 28

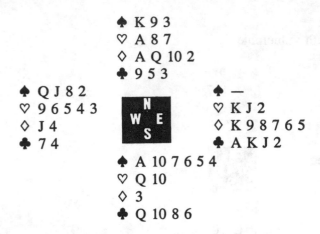

```
                    ♠ K 9 3
                    ♡ A 8 7
                    ◇ A Q 10 2
                    ♣ 9 5 3
  ♠ Q J 8 2                        ♠ —
  ♡ 9 6 5 4 3                      ♡ K J 2
  ◇ J 4                            ◇ K 9 8 7 6 5
  ♣ 7 4                            ♣ A K J 2
                    ♠ A 10 7 6 5 4
                    ♡ Q 10
                    ◇ 3
                    ♣ Q 10 8 6
```

South played in 3♠ after East had bid diamonds and clubs. West led the ◇ J, won by dummy's ace. Declarer played a low spade to the ace and a spade back to the king, West splitting his honours. The ◇ Q was covered and ruffed, and West was given the lead with the ♠ Q. A heart went to the king and the defence was still able to make two clubs and a trump, for one down.

South was pleased with himself, but North wondered why 3♠ had been defeated. "You knew the top clubs were on your right," he said. "You mustn't waste an entry by leading a trump at trick two. Play a club. The best they can do is take the club ruff. West exits with a heart. Now you go up with the ace, set up a diamond winner, then play ace and king of spades. You heart loser goes away on the ◇ 10. You lose just two clubs and two spades."

29 REPUTATION MISSED

Dealer South
North - South vulnerable

$$\spadesuit\ A$$
$$\heartsuit\ A\ K\ Q\ J$$
$$\diamondsuit\ K\ 10\ 5\ 2$$
$$\clubsuit\ Q\ 10\ 9\ 8$$

♠ K led

```
   N
 W   E
   S
```

$$\spadesuit\ 6\ 2$$
$$\heartsuit\ 5\ 2$$
$$\diamondsuit\ A\ 8\ 6\ 4\ 3$$
$$\clubsuit\ A\ J\ 7\ 6$$

South	West	North	East
Pass	4♠	Double	Pass
5◇	5♠	Double	Pass
6♣	Pass	6◇	Double
Pass	Pass	Pass	

South won the spade lead in dummy and after some thought advanced the ◇ K. When West showed out he had to go one down, even though the club finesse was right.

"I suppose I ought to have let them play in 5♠," said the declarer sadly. "As I had passed and held two aces, I thought we might be able to make a slam in one of my suits."

"The fact that you have passed doesn't make your hand any better," North replied. "You had a defensive type, really. But let me see. East was 2-3-4-4, wasn't he? Yes, I think you had a chance to make your reputation in this contract of 6◇."

"It's impossible to make it, if that's what you mean. East had ◇ Q J 9 7."

"Difficult; not impossible."

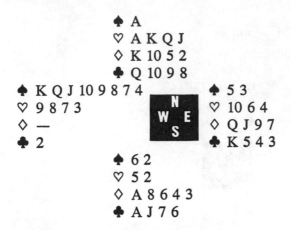

```
            ♠ A
            ♡ A K Q J
            ◇ K 10 5 2
            ♣ Q 10 9 8
♠ K Q J 10 9 8 7 4        ♠ 5 3
♡ 9 8 7 3                 ♡ 10 6 4
◇ —                       ◇ Q J 9 7
♣ 2                       ♣ K 5 4 3
            ♠ 6 2
            ♡ 5 2
            ◇ A 8 6 4 3
            ♣ A J 7 6
```

South played in 6 ◇ doubled after West had opened 4 ♠ and bid 5 ♠ on the next round. After winning the first trick South laid down the ◇ K and had no further chance.

"Even if East began with ◇ Q J 9 7 there may be a way to hold him to one trick," North explained. "Suppose you begin with the 10 from dummy. East covers and you win with the ace. You go to dummy with a heart and test the clubs. When the finesse wins you can see daylight. Take four clubs, ruff the third heart, and ruff your second spade in dummy. This leaves:

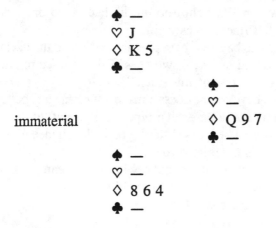

```
            ♠ —
            ♡ J
            ◇ K 5
            ♣ —
                          ♠ —
                          ♡ —
immaterial                ◇ Q 9 7
                          ♣ —
            ♠ —
            ♡ —
            ◇ 8 6 4
            ♣ —
```

"You're in dummy and you lead the ♡J. Quite simple, really."

Interlude for Defence

When we began this book we expected it to consist of problems for the declarer, but from time to time we came across interesting defensive problems, so we are breaking off now to present a few of these. The percipient player who so far has occupied the North position will sometimes be West, sometimes East.

30   HIGH BRANCHES

Dealer South
Neither side vulnerable

```
                        ♠ J 6 2
                        ♡ A K 7 5
                        ◇ K 9 6 2
                        ♣ A J
                                    ♠ 10 8 5 3
        ♣5 led        ┌─────┐      ♡ J 9 6 4 3
                      │  N  │      ◇ 8 5
                      │W   E│      ♣ K 4
                      │  S  │
                      └─────┘
```

South	West	North	East
1 ◇	Pass	2 ♡	Pass
3 ◇	Pass	4 ◇	Pass
4 NT	Pass	5 ◇	Pass
6 NT	Pass	Pass	Pass

Playing for a good score in a pairs event, North - South contracted for 6 NT rather than 6 ◇, which would have been easy.

West led the ♣5 and South played the jack from dummy, allowing East to win with the king. East returned the ♠3 and South won with the ace. He cashed a singleton ♡Q, crossed to the ◇K, and discarded a spade and a club on the top hearts. At the finish he held ♠J 6 and ♣A in dummy, ♠K and ♣9 7 in hand. West, holding control in both black suits, was squeezed.

"That's not good for us, is it?" said East. "Most pairs will be in 6 ◇."

"True, we had to beat 6 NT."

"Some pairs may miss the criss-cross squeeze."

"Yes, and some may encounter a better defence."

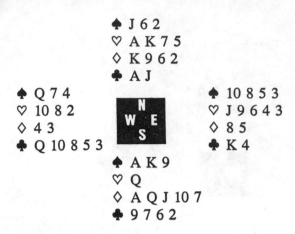

```
              ♠ J 6 2
              ♡ A K 7 5
              ◇ K 9 6 2
              ♣ A J
  ♠ Q 7 4                       ♠ 10 8 5 3
  ♡ 10 8 2         N            ♡ J 9 6 4 3
  ◇ 4 3         W     E         ◇ 8 5
  ♣ Q 10 8 5 3      S           ♣ K 4
              ♠ A K 9
              ♡ Q
              ◇ A Q J 10 7
              ♣ 9 7 6 2
```

North - South contracted for 6 NT. West led a low club; East won and returned the ♠3. South won with the ace and cashed his winners in the red suits. His last three cards were ♠J 6 and ♣A in dummy, ♠K and ♣9 7 in his own hand. West was unable to guard both black suits.

"What was the point of your spade return at trick two?" West demanded.

"I thought if I gave you the count in spades you wouldn't find it so difficult to keep the right cards."

"It wasn't difficult; it was impossible. You knew the hearts were no danger. You had to protect my hand from a squeeze in spades and clubs. It was essential to knock out the ♣A and not leave the declarer with top cards in each of those suits. Lop off the high branches by returning a club at trick two."

Dealer South
Game all

```
              ♠ Q 4
              ♡ A J 10 6 2
              ◇ J 8
              ♣ 8 7 5 3
♠ 10 8 5 2         N
♡ K 7          W       E
◇ K 7 5 2          S
♣ Q 9 4
```

South	West	North	East
1 ♠	Pass	1 NT	Pass
2 ♠	Pass	Pass	Double
3 ♠	Pass	Pass	Pass

West led a low diamond to the ace and East returned a low diamond, South playing the 9 and queen on these two tricks. West led a club to the ace and East returned a club. South won with the king and ran nine tricks — seven spades, one heart and one club.

"We could have made at least 4 ◇, but I hardly had enough to bid at that level," said West. "Also, I thought we might beat 3 ♠. Couldn't you have come in over 1 NT? You had good shape."

"I might have, but we were vulnerable, and I thought I'd see which way things were going," his partner replied. "Mind you, we could have beaten 3 ♠. It's a bit risky, but if you double we get a good result."

"How can we beat 3 ♠? Declarer had seven trump tricks, the ♡ A and the ♣ K."

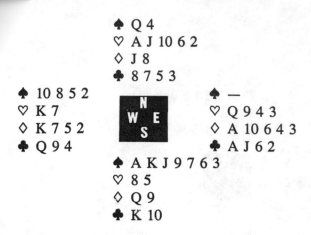

```
              ♠ Q 4
              ♡ A J 10 6 2
              ◇ J 8
              ♣ 8 7 5 3
♠ 10 8 5 2                    ♠ —
♡ K 7            N            ♡ Q 9 4 3
◇ K 7 5 2     W     E         ◇ A 10 6 4 3
♣ Q 9 4          S            ♣ A J 6 2
              ♠ A K J 9 7 6 3
              ♡ 8 5
              ◇ Q 9
              ♣ K 10
```

North - South had the better of the auction, obtaining the contract in 3♠. The defence made the ace and king of diamonds, then West led a club and East returned a club. Now South had nine tricks on top.

"Your club lead wasn't very dynamic," East remarked. "After the two diamonds you must switch to the ♡K. South wins and leads a club. I go up with the ace and play queen and another heart, establishing a trump trick for our side."

32 WRONG EXIT

Dealer South
Both sides vulnerable

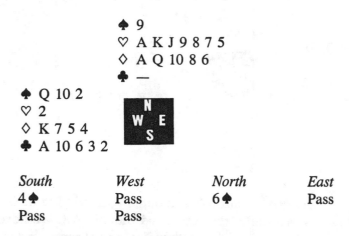

♠ 9
♡ A K J 9 8 7 5
◊ A Q 10 8 6
♣ —

♠ Q 10 2
♡ 2
◊ K 7 5 4
♣ A 10 6 3 2

South	West	North	East
4♠	Pass	6♠	Pass
Pass	Pass		

West led the ♣A. Dummy ruffed, East played the king and South the 5. Declarer played the ♡A, then another heart, which he ruffed with the ♠8. West overruffed and tried a second club, but South ruffed and made the rest of the tricks.

"South might have had another club," said West. "Anyway, there was nothing we could do."

"If South had held another club he would have tried to discard it on the hearts, I imagine," East replied. "There was only one real chance, and it would have worked "

Replay of 32

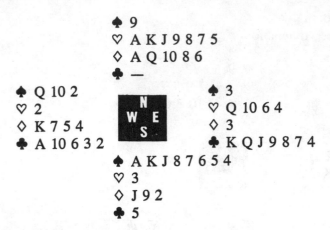

```
                ♠ 9
                ♡ A K J 9 8 7 5
                ◇ A Q 10 8 6
                ♣ —
♠ Q 10 2                          ♠ 3
♡ 2              N                ♡ Q 10 6 4
◇ K 7 5 4     W     E             ◇ 3
♣ A 10 6 3 2     S               ♣ K Q J 9 8 7 4
                ♠ A K J 8 7 6 5 4
                ♡ 3
                ◇ J 9 2
                ♣ 5
```

West led the ♣A against 6♠ and dummy ruffed. The declarer cashed the ♡A and ruffed the next round with the ♠8. West over-ruffed and tried a second club. South ruffed, drew trumps, and took the winning finesse in diamonds.

"You could hardly expect to make another trick in clubs," East informed his partner. "With a doubleton club South would have played for a discard on the ♡K. With a singleton diamond and three clubs he would have come to hand with a diamond ruff, cashed the top spades, and played for discards on the hearts. When you over-ruffed the second heart you had to return the ◇K."

33 A QUESTION OF CONTROL

Dealer South
Both sides vulnerable

```
                    ♠ 6 4
                    ♡ K Q 5 2
                    ♢ 6 3
                    ♣ A Q 8 7 5
                                    ♠ 7 5 2
   ♡J led              N             ♡ A 8 6 4 3
                    W     E          ♢ 7 4
                      S              ♣ K 10 3
```

South	West	North	East
1 ♢	Pass	2 ♣	Pass
2 ♠	Pass	2 NT	Pass
3 ♠	Pass	3 NT	Pass
4 ♢	Pass	4 ♠	Pass
Pass	Pass		

The ♡J was covered by the queen and ace, and South ruffed. He followed with ace, king and another diamond, West turning up with Q 10 5. Dummy ruffed the third diamond and East overruffed. East returned a heart, on which South discarded a club. Now a spade to the queen lost to the king. West played a heart, South ruffed and cashed the ♠A. The rest of his hand was high except for the ♠J.

"That was a lucky contract," East exclaimed. "Your trumps were A Q 10 x x opposite two small."

"Yes, we ought to have been in 5 ♢, I suppose," said South. "Still, 620's better than 600, isn't it?"

"I don't know how you made 4 ♠," said West. "Ah, wait a minute. Yes, we could have beaten it even after the heart lead."

Replay of 33

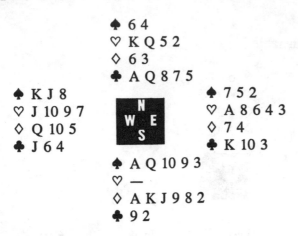

♠ 6 4
♡ K Q 5 2
◇ 6 3
♣ A Q 8 7 5

♠ K J 8
♡ J 10 9 7
◇ Q 10 5
♣ J 6 4

♠ 7 5 2
♡ A 8 6 4 3
◇ 7 4
♣ K 10 3

♠ A Q 10 9 3
♡ —
◇ A K J 9 8 2
♣ 9 2

North - South finished in a perilous contract of 4♠ after South had shown longer diamonds than spades. The ♡J was covered by the queen and ace, and South ruffed. East overruffed the dummy on the third round of diamonds and returned a heart. West made two spade tricks, but South had the tempo.

"That was a most unusual hand," West observed. "Though it seemed natural, your overruff of the dummy was a mistake. So long as we both keep three trumps, we are in control. South was already down to four trumps, remember. If you let him ruff the third diamond, what can he do next? He finesses in trumps, I win and play a club or a heart. He must shorten himself again to recover the lead, and by that time he has only two trumps and we have two each."

Dealer South
Both sides vulnerable

                    ♠ A K 8 4 3
                    ♡ K 4
                    ◇ J 3
                    ♣ Q 10 6 3

    ♠ 10 7 6 2
    ♡ J 3   N
    ◇ 6 4   W   E
    ♣ A K 8 7 4   S

South	West	North	East
1 ◇	Pass	1 ♠	Pass
2 ♡	Pass	3 NT	Pass
4 ♡	Pass	5 ◇	Pass
6 ◇	Pass	Pass	Pass

West led the ♣A, on which his partner played the 2 and declarer the 5. To prevent possible heart ruffs, West switched to the ◇4. South won in hand, played king, ace and another heart, ruffing in dummy, then ruffed a club. Five more rounds of diamonds followed and the defence was much embarrassed, since West had to keep the ♣K and East the ♡Q. Both defenders unguarded spades, and the declarer made the last three tricks in this suit.

"There was nothing we could do," said West. "I had to lead a trump at trick two to prevent heart ruffs."

"Really, the defence wasn't difficult," said East crossly. "You knew South's exact shape from the bidding and the play to the first trick."

Replay of 34

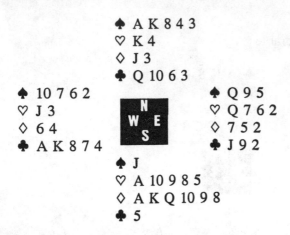

```
              ♠ A K 8 4 3
              ♡ K 4
              ◇ J 3
              ♣ Q 10 6 3
♠ 10 7 6 2              ♠ Q 9 5
♡ J 3          N        ♡ Q 7 6 2
◇ 6 4        W   E      ◇ 7 5 2
♣ A K 8 7 4    S        ♣ J 9 2
              ♠ J
              ♡ A 10 9 8 5
              ◇ A K Q 10 9 8
              ♣ 5
```

South played in 6◇ after bidding that suggested 5-6 in the red suits. West led the ♣A and switched to a trump. Declarer ruffed the third round of hearts, came back with a club ruff, and played off all the trumps. At the end there was a double squeeze, and dummy made the last three tricks in spades.

"What was the point of your trump switch?" East demanded.

"To prevent heart ruffs, of course."

"You had the 6 4 of trumps, dummy the J 3. He could only ruff once, because on the third heart you would insert the 4 of diamonds. It was essential to play a spade at trick two, to destroy the entry for a possible double squeeze."

35 STILL ASLEEP

Dealer West
Neither side vulnerable

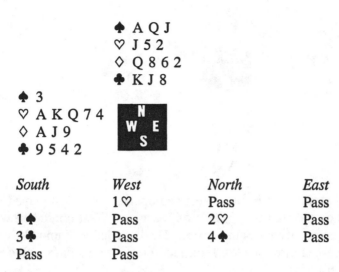

```
              ♠ A Q J
              ♡ J 5 2
              ◇ Q 8 6 2
              ♣ K J 8
♠ 3
♡ A K Q 7 4      N
◇ A J 9        W   E
♣ 9 5 4 2        S
```

South	West	North	East
	1♡	Pass	Pass
1♠	Pass	2♡	Pass
3♣	Pass	4♠	Pass
Pass	Pass		

Since players tend to reopen on rather weak hands these days, North advanced cautiously in preference to raising to 3♠. The rebid of 3♣ appeared to improve his hand.

West led the ♡K, on which East played the 8 and declarer the 6. On the next heart East dropped the 9 and South the 10. As his partner seemed to want a heart continuation, West led a third round, which was ruffed by South.

Declarer played a low diamond to the queen, cashed three top spades in dummy, then crossed to a high club and drew the last trump. He made game with five tricks in spades, four in clubs and one in diamonds."

"Did you enjoy your rest?" asked East.

"What do you mean? There was nothing I could do."

Replay of 35

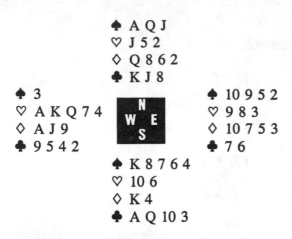

```
              ♠ A Q J
              ♡ J 5 2
              ◇ Q 8 6 2
              ♣ K J 8
♠ 3                           ♠ 10 9 5 2
♡ A K Q 7 4      N            ♡ 9 8 3
◇ A J 9        W   E          ◇ 10 7 5 3
♣ 9 5 4 2        S            ♣ 7 6
              ♠ K 8 7 6 4
              ♡ 10 6
              ◇ K 4
              ♣ A Q 10 3
```

South played in 4♠ after West had opened 1♡. East played the 8 and 9 on the first two rounds of hearts, so West continued with a third round, which South ruffed. Declarer led a diamond to the queen, cashed three spades, returned to hand with a club, and drew the last trump.

"You played the ♡8 on the first round, so I assumed you wanted me to continue the suit," said West. "Anyway, there was no defence."

"Certainly I wanted you to press on in hearts. It might have occurred to you that I held four trumps. Evidently it occurred to the declarer, because it was good play by him to lead a diamond before drawing trumps. You had to go up with the ace and lead a fourth heart, on which I throw a club. That kills him."

36 FALSE ENCOURAGEMENT

Dealer South
North - South vulnerable

```
                    ♠ 8 7 4
                    ♡ A 10 6 4 2
                    ◊ K 7 3
                    ♣ J 5
      ♠ 9 6 5 2          N
      ♡ J 9 7 5       W     E
      ◊ A 10             S
      ♣ 8 7 4
```

South	West	North	East
1 NT	Pass	2 ◊	Pass
2 ♡	Pass	2 NT	Pass
3 ♡	Pass	3 NT	Pass
Pass	Pass		

North - South were playing a 15-17 notrump and North's 2 ◊ was a transfer to hearts.

West led the ♣8, which turned out to be a good choice. South played the jack from dummy and East covered with the queen, which held. East returned the ♣10 and South won with the king.

South played king, queen and 8 of hearts, running five tricks in the suit. East, who had to make four discards, chose three diamonds and a spade. South, who held A Q J of spades, finessed the queen and followed with the ace, thus making nine tricks.

"Did you have to unguard the ♠K?" West asked his partner.

"Yes, I was squeezed on the last heart," said East. "If I throw a club declarer can drive out the ace of diamonds, and if I throw my fourth diamond he can finesse in spades and throw me in with a club. I was 3-1-4-5. Funnily enough, I think that our best chance to beat the contract lay with you."

"What could I have done?" West asked in an unbelieving tone.

Replay of 36

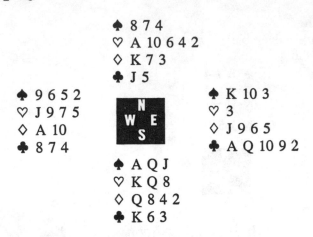

```
             ♠ 8 7 4
             ♡ A 10 6 4 2
             ◇ K 7 3
             ♣ J 5
♠ 9 6 5 2                    ♠ K 10 3
♡ J 9 7 5        N           ♡ 3
◇ A 10        W   E          ◇ J 9 6 5
♣ 8 7 4          S           ♣ A Q 10 9 2
             ♠ A Q J
             ♡ K Q 8
             ◇ Q 8 4 2
             ♣ K 6 3
```

South played in 3 NT after showing some support for hearts. West led the ♣8, East held the trick with the queen and returned the 10. South ran five heart tricks, destroying the East hand. On the last heart East discarded a spade. South then finessed the ♠Q and brought down the king on the next round.

West was very surprised when East observed that he, West, had the only chance to beat the contract.

"You knew the heart position after the first round," said East. "Your hearts were dead and it would have been a clever move to drop the jack under the queen on the second round. South will assume that you hold J x and will overtake with the ace so that he can finesse the ♠Q, return to the ♡10 and later finesse again in spades. But of course the hearts won't be good and we will easily beat the contract."

37 THROUGH THE SLIPS

Dealer West
Neither side vulnerable

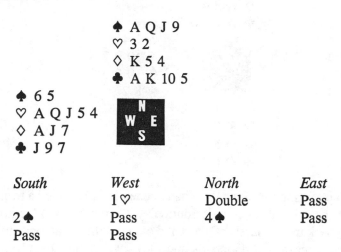

♠ A Q J 9
♡ 3 2
◇ K 5 4
♣ A K 10 5

♠ 6 5
♡ A Q J 5 4
◇ A J 7
♣ J 9 7

South	West	North	East
	1 ♡	Double	Pass
2 ♠	Pass	4 ♠	Pass
Pass	Pass		

West led a trump and declarer drew three rounds. East followed suit and West discarded a heart. South led a diamond to the king, then played three top clubs, East discarding a diamond on the third round. Now a diamond ran to the jack. West cashed the two red aces, then had to give South a trick with the ♡K.

"You weren't much help there," West remarked to his partner.

"I had enough to beat them, as a matter of fact," East replied. "If you had been awake, that is."

```
                    ♠ A Q J 9
                    ♡ 3 2
                    ◇ K 5 4
                    ♣ A K 10 5
   ♠ 6 5                            ♠ 7 4 3
   ♡ A Q J 5 4        N             ♡ 10 9 7 6
   ◇ A J 7          W   E           ◇ 10 9 3 2
   ♣ J 9 7            S             ♣ 8 2
                    ♠ K 10 8 2
                    ♡ K 8
                    ◇ Q 8 6
                    ♣ Q 6 4 3
```

South played in 4♠ after West had opened 1♡. West led a trump, and after drawing three rounds South played a diamond to the king. Then he took three rounds of clubs and exited with a diamond, forcing West to cash two diamonds and play away from the ♡A.

"I had the 10 9 of both red suits," East pointed out. "That's enough, so long as you unblock the ◇J on the first round."

"How could I do that?" West protested. "For all I knew, you might have held an entry in clubs."

"So? A club, two hearts and a diamond would be enough, wouldn't it?"

"You could have had the ♡K and something like 10 x x in diamonds; or even 10 x alone."

"All this is a bit unlikely. If South had held long diamonds and the ♣Q he would have played for a discard on dummy's clubs. Also, I passed over North's double on the first round, so I couldn't hold as much as king to four hearts and the ♣Q. The best chance was to play me for 10 9 in both red suits."

38   NEXT ROUND

Dealer South
North - South vulnerable

```
              ♠ A 4 2
              ♡ 9 6 3
              ◇ J 10 8 7 6
              ♣ 9 5
  ♠ K Q 8 6        N
  ♡ K 5 4      W       E
  ◇ K 5           S
  ♣ A 7 6 2
```

South	West	North	East
1♡	Double	Pass	1♠
2♣	2♠	3♡	3♠
4♡	4♠	Pass	Pass
5♡	Double	Pass	Pass
Pass			

West led the ♠K to dummy's ace, and the ♣5 was covered by
the 8, queen and ace. West led another spade, which South ruffed.
Declarer cashed the ♡A, on which East's queen fell, then played
a high club, followed by a low club, which was ruffed in dummy.
A heart went to West's king, but that was the end of the defence,
as declarer held the singleton ◇A.

"I thought we were sure to beat that when I saw the dummy,"
said West.

"South was quite likely to be 6-5, wasn't he?" said East. "You
couldn't rely on a trick in spades or diamonds. Still, if you play sensibly, we can still get them down one."

"If I begin with a low heart, do you mean? As you had the queen,
we can get in three rounds of trumps."

"That's true, but I was thinking of a defence after you had begun
with the ♠K."

Replay of 38

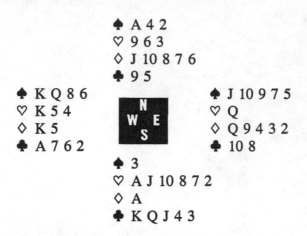

♠ A 4 2
♡ 9 6 3
◇ J 10 8 7 6
♣ 9 5

♠ K Q 8 6
♡ K 5 4
◇ K 5
♣ A 7 6 2

♠ J 10 9 7 5
♡ Q
◇ Q 9 4 3 2
♣ 10 8

♠ 3
♡ A J 10 8 7 2
◇ A
♣ K Q J 4 3

South played in 5 ♡ doubled after a competitive auction in which he had shown length in hearts and clubs. South won the spade lead in dummy and played a club, which went to the 8, queen and ace. West led another spade. South ruffed, cash the ♡A, played the ♣K and ruffed a club. He lost only to the ♡K and the ♣A.

"As you say, you might have led a trump," said East, "but that works well only because I held the queen. The mistake was in winning the first round of clubs. If South plays a second high club you can win and give me a ruff with the ♡Q. It doesn't help declarer to cash the ♡A, because then you can play king and another heart when you come in with the ♣A."

39 DIFFERENT MISTAKE

Dealer South
East - West vulnerable

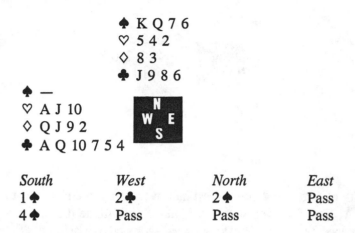

```
              ♠ K Q 7 6
              ♡ 5 4 2
              ◇ 8 3
              ♣ J 9 8 6
♠ —
♡ A J 10         N
◇ Q J 9 2      W   E
♣ A Q 10 7 5 4   S
```

South	West	North	East
1♠	2♣	2♠	Pass
4♠	Pass	Pass	Pass

West led the ♣A, East played the 3 and South the king. West switched to the ◇Q. South won with the ace, drew trumps in three rounds, and cashed the ◇K. Then he produced the ♣2, to West's annoyance. When he won with the queen, West could see that a club lead would give dummy an extra club trick and a diamond would allow a ruff-and-discard. He played the ♡10, therefore. As expected, South held the king, and declarer's third heart went away on the ♣J.

"Sorry about that," said West. "It really looked as though your ♣3 was from 3 2. If I give you a club ruff you return the ♡Q and we get it two down."

"I don't blame you at all," said East. "I mean, I don't blame you for not leading a second club, which might have been fatal. But you lost your head later."

Replay of 39

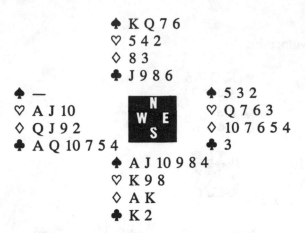

```
              ♠ K Q 7 6
              ♡ 5 4 2
              ◊ 8 3
              ♣ J 9 8 6
♠ —                        ♠ 5 3 2
♡ A J 10      N            ♡ Q 7 6 3
◊ Q J 9 2   W   E          ◊ 10 7 6 5 4
♣ A Q 10 7 5 4  S          ♣ 3
              ♠ A J 10 9 8 4
              ♡ K 9 8
              ◊ A K
              ♣ K 2
```

South played in 4♠ after West had overcalled in clubs. West led the ♣A, East followed with the 3, and South made the fairly well known deceptive play of the king. West switched to a diamond. South now drew trumps, cashed the second diamond, and led the ♣2. West took the queen and tried a heart, but South held the king and a third heart went away on the ♣J.

"It was difficult for you to play a low club at trick two, I agree," said East. "Actually the ♡J gets them one down, but that might have been wrong too. The mistake came later when South eliminated the diamonds and led a second club. You must play low. He wins with the 9 and leads a heart from dummy. We then take three heart tricks."

"Only if you go up with the queen."

"I might have managed that," said East dryly.

Back on the Track

We return now to problems for the declarer. There is no intended difference between the problems in this group and those in the first set.

40 TAKING THE CUE

Dealer South
East - West vulnerable

                    ♠ A 5
                    ♡ J 7 5
                    ◇ A 6 4 3
                    ♣ K J 10 8

    ♡ 10 led   N
                   W   E
                      S

                    ♠ K Q J 4 2
                    ♡ 4 3
                    ◇ K 9 8
                    ♣ A Q 9

South	West	North	East
1 ♠	Pass	2 ♣	Pass
3 ♣	Pass	3 ◇	Pass
3 ♠	Pass	4 ♠	Double
Pass	Pass	Pass	

West led the ♡ 10 and East played off three top hearts. As South had no loser to throw and could not afford to lose this trick if the trumps were 5-1, he ruffed and played ace and another spade. As feared, East did not follow. The only hope now was that the player with the five trumps would not hold another heart. But West was 5-4 in the majors and South finished one down, losing in effect one trump and three hearts.

"I thought the trumps might be 5-1 but there was nothing I could do," said the declarer.

"If you realized that the trumps were likely to be breaking badly, you might have adopted a different plan," his partner replied.

Replay of 40

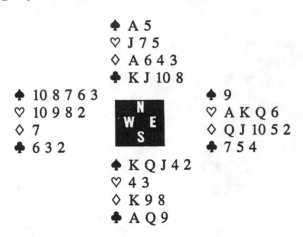

```
              ♠ A 5
              ♡ J 7 5
              ◊ A 6 4 3
              ♣ K J 10 8
♠ 10 8 7 6 3              ♠ 9
♡ 10 9 8 2    N          ♡ A K Q 6
◊ 7         W   E        ◊ Q J 10 5 2
♣ 6 3 2       S          ♣ 7 5 4
              ♠ K Q J 4 2
              ♡ 4 3
              ◊ K 9 8
              ♣ A Q 9
```

When North - South bid to 4♠ in a manner that suggested the trumps were not strongly held, East made an imaginative double. This is quite a common manoeuvre among good players when they hold a few tricks and judge that their partners are long in trumps. West intelligently led a heart in preference to his singleton diamond. South ruffed the third round, played ace and another spade, and had to concede one down when West turned up with the long trump and a winning heart.

"Why do you suppose East doubled?" North demanded. "He had to be either very long or very short in trumps."

"I know that," said South, "but I had to ruff the third heart and this left West with the long trump. The only chance was that he had no more hearts."

"Not the only chance at all. After the ♠A play on clubs. It's not fatal if a defender who began with five trumps ruffs a club. As it happens, they both follow to three rounds. You play a fourth club, discarding a diamond from hand. All they make is their long trump."

41 FORCE OF HABIT

Dealer South
Both sides vulnerable

```
                    ♠ 3 2
                    ♡ J 7 5 4
                    ◇ A J 2
                    ♣ 7 6 4 2
   ♡A led        ┌─────────┐
                 │    N    │
                 │  W   E  │
                 │    S    │
                 └─────────┘
                    ♠ A K Q 8 7
                    ♡ 3
                    ◇ Q 7 5
                    ♣ A Q 9 8
```

South	West	North	East
1♠	Pass	1 NT	2♡
3♣	Pass	4♣	Pass
5♣	Pass	Pass	Pass

The final contract was insecure because North's raise was borderline at best. South's 3♣ bid, in the competitive sequence, should not be regarded as forcing. North might have passed.

West led the ♡A and switched to the ◇9. South let this run to the queen, then led a second diamond to the jack. Disaster struck. East ruffed and led the ♡Q. South ruffed with the queen of trumps and played ace and another. All followed, but he was one down.

"We both pushed a bit too hard there," South remarked. "Still, it was unlucky to run into a 6-1 diamond break."

"It was a doubtful contract, I agree. But you could have made it easily enough."

Replay of 41

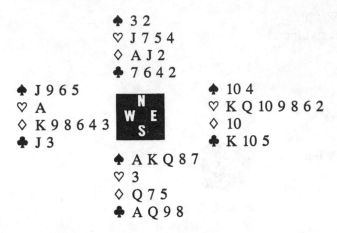

```
              ♠ 3 2
              ♡ J 7 5 4
              ◊ A J 2
              ♣ 7 6 4 2
♠ J 9 6 5                    ♠ 10 4
♡ A               N          ♡ K Q 10 9 8 6 2
◊ K 9 8 6 4 3   W   E        ◊ 10
♣ J 3               S        ♣ K 10 5
              ♠ A K Q 8 7
              ♡ 3
              ◊ Q 7 5
              ♣ A Q 9 8
```

North - South reached a borderline 5♣ after East had overcalled in hearts. West cashed the ♡A and switched to the ◊9. South let this run to the queen and led a second round to the jack, as his general plan was to finesse in clubs and aim to lose just one heart and one club. However, East ruffed the second diamond and led the ♡Q. South did the best he could now, ruffing with the queen and playing ace and another club, to go one down.

"Does it make any difference if I play off the ♣A?" South asked.

"No. What you might have done was insert dummy's ◊J at trick two. Then you finesse the ♣Q, cash the ace, and lose just to the ♣K."

42 PARTIAL RECOVERY

Dealer East
North - South vulnerable

```
              ♠ 10 9 2
              ♡ A 10 5
              ◊ A K 9 3 2
              ♣ K 2

♠4 led          N
             W     E
                S

              ♠ A Q 3
              ♡ K J 9 8 7 6 2
              ◊ —
              ♣ J 7 6
```

South	West	North	East
			1♠
2♡	Pass	2♠	Double
3♡	Pass	5♡	Pass
6♡	Pass	Pass	Pass

West led the ♠4, which was covered by the 9, jack and queen. After some thought the declarer led a heart to dummy's ace, on which East showed out. South made a partial recovery by playing ace, king, and another diamond, discarding three clubs and allowing East to hold the trick. East was on play now: a spade would take his partner's trump trick; a club would be ruffed and would establish a trick for dummy's king; and a diamond would make it possible for South to establish a diamond trick for the discard of his spade loser, the ♡10 providing an entry.

"I know what you're going to say," said South. "If I play the ♡K first I can pick up the trumps as the cards lie, but there still aren't enough entries for me to establish an extra diamond trick. I was hoping for a single ♡Q, which would provide me with three trump entries to the dummy."

"I see that," said North "But it's still right to begin with the ♡K."

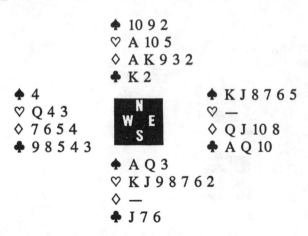

- ♠ 10 9 2
- ♡ A 10 5
- ◊ A K 9 3 2
- ♣ K 2

- ♠ 4
- ♡ Q 4 3
- ◊ 7 6 5 4
- ♣ 9 8 5 4 3

- ♠ K J 8 7 6 5
- ♡ —
- ◊ Q J 10 8
- ♣ A Q 10

- ♠ A Q 3
- ♡ K J 9 8 7 6 2
- ◊ —
- ♣ J 7 6

South played in 6 ♡ after East had overcalled in spades. Since East had made a rather pointless double of North's 2 ♠ and had not doubled the final contract, West led his singleton spade rather than a club. South won and began with a heart to the ace. After that, the best he could do was let East win the third round of diamonds, while he discarded three clubs from his own hand.

South explained that he had thought of beginning with the ♡ K, but his plan was to enter dummy three times in the trump suit and establish a diamond winner for a discard.

"It was more likely that West, rather than East, would hold three hearts, wasn't it?" said North, "and in any case your plan succeeds only if you bring down a singleton queen. Why not begin with the ♡ K? You pick up the queen, discard two clubs on the top diamonds, and end-play East, who has to come down at the finish to two spades and the ♣ A."

43 MORE TROUBLE

Dealer South
East - West vulnerable

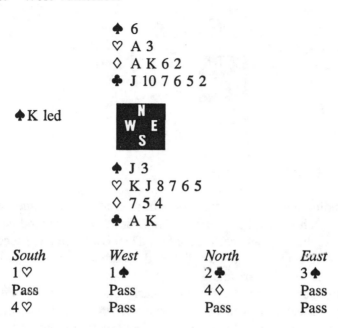

```
              ♠ 6
              ♡ A 3
              ◇ A K 6 2
              ♣ J 10 7 6 5 2
♠ K led
              ♠ J 3
              ♡ K J 8 7 6 5
              ◇ 7 5 4
              ♣ A K
```

South	West	North	East
1♡	1♠	2♣	3♠
Pass	Pass	4◇	Pass
4♡	Pass	Pass	Pass

West led the ♠K and switched to a trump, which ran to the queen and king. Expecting to make overtricks, South led a heart to the ace, on which West showed out. Declarer came back with a club, cashed the ♡J, and then led a second club. More trouble: East ruffed with his remaining trump, cashed a spade, and led a diamond. Suddenly it was impossible to make even ten tricks.

South had a feeling that he might have done better. "Perhaps I should have gone up with the ♡A and ruffed my low spade," he suggested.

"That doesn't make any difference," North replied. "You gain a trick in spades, lose a trick in trumps. There's a better plan than that."

Replay of 43

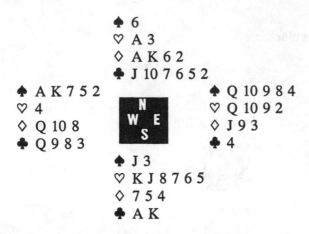

```
              ♠ 6
              ♡ A 3
              ◇ A K 6 2
              ♣ J 10 7 6 5 2
♠ A K 7 5 2                    ♠ Q 10 9 8 4
♡ 4              N            ♡ Q 10 9 2
◇ Q 10 8      W     E         ◇ J 9 3
♣ Q 9 8 3         S           ♣ 4
              ♠ J 3
              ♡ K J 8 7 6 5
              ◇ 7 5 4
              ♣ A K
```

Defending against 4♡, West led a high spade and switched to a trump, which ran to the queen and king. South led a second heart, returned to the ♣A, and cashed the ♡J. Then East ruffed the second club, cashed a spade, and led a diamond. South was one down, losing two spades, a heart and a diamond.

"It's better play to test the clubs early on," North explained. "When you come in with the ♡K, play off ♣A K. If they break 4-1, as they do, you still have plenty of entries to the dummy. Say that East ruffs the second club and leads a spade; you ruff in dummy and have enough entries to set up the clubs."

"I suppose that's right," said South. "But suppose East throws a diamond instead of ruffing the second club."

"No difference; one way is to cross to the ♡A, lead the ♣J and discard your spade loser."

44 REMOVE THE OBSTRUCTION

Dealer North
Neither side vulnerable

♠ 8 7 5 4
♡ A Q 8 5 2
◊ K 7
♣ A K

♣ 10 led

```
 N
W   E
 S
```

♠ Q
♡ K 10 4
◊ A 10 9 8 6 3
♣ Q J 2

South	West	North	East
		1 ♡	4 ♠
5 ◊	Pass	6 ◊	Pass
Pass	Pass		

South had an awkward decision over East's 4 ♠. 5 ♡, 5 ◊ and double were all possible choices. When South bid 5 ◊ it seemed to North that he had at least four very important cards.

Declarer won the club lead in dummy. When ◊ K was led East followed with the queen but on the second round of trumps he discarded a spade. West won the third round of trumps and played another club to dummy's king. South came to hand with the ♡ K, drew the last trump, and led the ♡ 10. West, who had begun with ♡ J 9 x x, covered with the jack. Now declarer was in the wrong hand, unable to return for a finesse of the ♡ 8. He had to lose a spade.

"I didn't want to be in six," South remarked a little sulkily. "I had to say something over 4 ♠."

"I'm sorry about that," said North. "I had some good cards, I thought. And I've an idea you might have made it."

Replay of 44

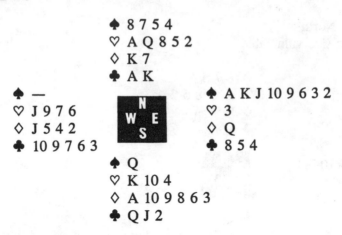

```
              ♠ 8 7 5 4
              ♡ A Q 8 5 2
              ◇ K 7
              ♣ A K
♠ —                          ♠ A K J 10 9 6 3 2
♡ J 9 7 6        N           ♡ 3
◇ J 5 4 2    W     E         ◇ Q
♣ 10 9 7 6 3     S           ♣ 8 5 4
              ♠ Q
              ♡ K 10 4
              ◇ A 10 9 8 6 3
              ♣ Q J 2
```

A jump overcall of 4♠ by East left North - South with little bidding space and they finished in 6◇. South won the club lead in dummy and played three rounds of diamonds. West exited with a second club. South came to hand with a heart and drew the last trump, but then the ♡10 was covered by the jack and declarer was stranded in dummy. He had to give up a spade at the finish.

"I don't see how I could have made it," said South. "I knew West was void of spades, of course, but the entries were awkward and I couldn't get back to finesse the ♡8."

"By the time West won with the ◇J you knew that East had four cards between hearts and clubs," North pointed out. "Isn't it safe to discard the ♣K on the third diamond, to avoid having to win the next club in dummy? West exits with a club, which you win with the queen. After drawing the last trump you can lead the third club. When East follows, the hearts must be 4-1 and the odds must favour the lead of the ♡10 on the first round."

45 TEST CASE

Dealer South
Neither side vulnerable

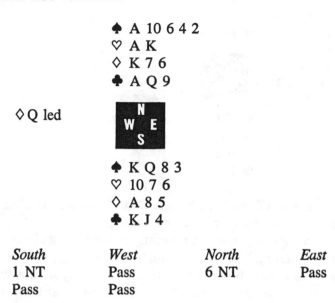

♦ Q led

◆ A 10 6 4 2
♡ A K
◊ K 7 6
♣ A Q 9

◆ K Q 8 3
♡ 10 7 6
◊ A 8 5
♣ K J 4

South	West	North	East
1 NT	Pass	6 NT	Pass
Pass	Pass		

West led the ◊ Q. South won and laid down the ♠K. Unfortunately, West showed out. South gave up a spade and tried for a squeeze, but prospects for this were slim and he finished one down.

"I know I could have played the spades the other way — ace first — but there wasn't any indication," South declared. "I don't know why you didn't give me a Stayman 2♣. We had nine spades between us."

"I know, but you can't take any ruffs in the short hand, so playing in spades doesn't help. As a rule, on this type of hand, it is a mistake to follow a sequence that will help the opposition to assess your distribution. And 6 NT, as it happens, is a better contract. If you play correctly you make it."

Replay of 45

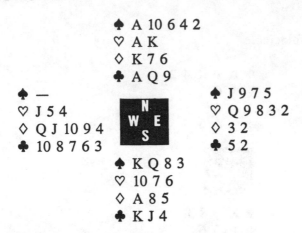

```
                    ♠ A 10 6 4 2
                    ♡ A K
                    ◇ K 7 6
                    ♣ A Q 9
    ♠ —                              ♠ J 9 7 5
    ♡ J 5 4          N               ♡ Q 9 8 3 2
    ◇ Q J 10 9 4   W   E             ◇ 3 2
    ♣ 10 8 7 6 3     S               ♣ 5 2
                    ♠ K Q 8 3
                    ♡ 10 7 6
                    ◇ A 8 5
                    ♣ K J 4
```

South was in 6 NT and West led the ◇ Q. South won and led the
♠ K. After this he had no real chance for the contract.

"The advantage of playing in notrump," North pointed out, "is
that when you have a long suit that can be played in more than one
way you can postpone the decision. If you were playing this hand
in spades, obviously you would have to play trumps at trick two.
Playing in notrumps, I think you should duck the first diamond. Later,
you play two more rounds of diamonds and three rounds of clubs.
You soon find out that East has a doubleton in both minors, so it's
not difficult to read him for the likely length in spades. As you still
have two heart entries in dummy, you can pick up East's spades
and return to make the fifth spade."

46 SLIGHT HAZARD

Dealer South
North - South vulnerable

```
              ♠ 2
              ♡ A K 3
              ◊ J 9 5
              ♣ A K 7 6 4 2

  ♡ 10 led        N
                W   E
                  S

              ♠ A Q J 9 8 6
              ♡ 7 5 2
              ◊ A 10 7
              ♣ 3
```

South	West	North	East
1♠	Pass	2♣	Pass
2♠	Pass	3♡	Pass
3♠	Pass	4♠	Pass
Pass	Pass		

South won the heart lead in dummy and finessed the ♠Q, losing to the king. West led a second heart and after taking this trick South discarded his third heart on the ♣K. He tried the ◊J from dummy, but there was no cover and he lost to West's queen. West exited with a third heart and when the spades broke 4-2 South was one down, losing two spades and two diamonds.

"That was typical," said South. "Four spades to the K 10 sitting over me."

"I don't think you played for the best chance," replied his partner.

Replay of 46

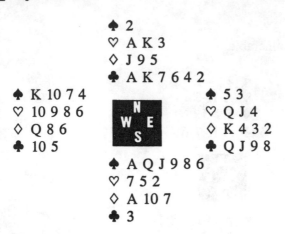

```
              ♠ 2
              ♡ A K 3
              ◇ J 9 5
              ♣ A K 7 6 4 2
♠ K 10 7 4              ♠ 5 3
♡ 10 9 8 6      N       ♡ Q J 4
◇ Q 8 6      W   E      ◇ K 4 3 2
♣ 10 5          S       ♣ Q J 9 8
              ♠ A Q J 9 8 6
              ♡ 7 5 2
              ◇ A 10 7
              ♣ 3
```

Playing in 4♠, South won the heart lead in dummy and lost a spade finesse to the king. West led a second heart and South took a discard on the second round of clubs. Then he led the ◇ J, but East declined to cover. West won and exited with a heart. When he won the fourth round of spades West was able to exit with a fourth heart, and South still had to lose another diamond.

"You didn't make the best use of dummy's entries," North pointed out. "Leading a trump from the table, as opposed to playing ace and queen from hand, gains only when East has K x. It is much better to give yourself the best chance of two tricks in diamonds. Leading only once towards the A 10 7, as you did, will be good enough only if East holds K Q or possibly a doubleton honour. True, there are slight hazards in not leading a trump early on, but the diamond play is certainly best."

47 EYE ON THE BALL

Dealer South
North - South vulnerable

```
              ♠ 8 4 3 2
              ♡ A 2
              ◇ Q J 7 6
              ♣ Q 5 2
  ♣ 8 led       N
            W       E
                S
              ♠ A J 10 7
              ♡ Q 5 4
              ◇ A 10
              ♣ K J 9 4
```

South	West	North	East
1♣	Pass	1◇	Pass
1♠	Pass	2♠	Pass
Pass	Pass		

East won the club lead and returned the 6 of trumps. South's 10 lost to the queen and West switched to a low heart, which was won by East's king. East returned a diamond and the finesse lost. As West turned out to hold K Q 9 5 of spades, the defence made three tricks in spades and one in each of the other suits, defeating the contract.

"We didn't do badly there," said South complacently. "I nearly bid again over your 2♠. We might have finished in 4♠ doubled and lost 800."

"Maybe," said North, "but as you were in 2♠ only, why not play safe and make it?"

"I don't see what else I could have done," replied South indignantly.

Replay of 47

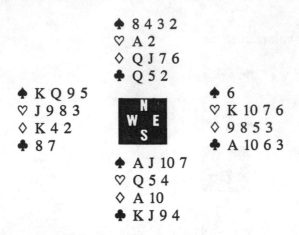

```
                 ♠ 8 4 3 2
                 ♡ A 2
                 ◊ Q J 7 6
                 ♣ Q 5 2
 ♠ K Q 9 5            N            ♠ 6
 ♡ J 9 8 3        W       E        ♡ K 10 7 6
 ◊ K 4 2             S             ◊ 9 8 5 3
 ♣ 8 7                             ♣ A 10 6 3
                 ♠ A J 10 7
                 ♡ Q 5 4
                 ◊ A 10
                 ♣ K J 9 4
```

South played in 2 ♠ and West led a club. East won and returned a trump, which ran to the 10 and queen. Then a heart went to the king, the diamond finesse lost, and the defence took two more tricks in the trump suit.

South thought he had done well to stop in 2 ♠, with the cards lying so badly, but North was not satisfied.

"You could afford to lose three trump tricks," he pointed out. "Why not go up with the ♠A at trick two? Then you can either discard a heart from dummy on the fourth club, or you can give up a diamond and discard two hearts on ◊ Q J. Either way, you lose just three spades, a diamond and a club."

Dealer South
Both sides vulnerable

           ♠ A 7 6 5 4
           ♡ 2
           ◊ K 9 7 4 2
           ♣ K 3

◊ Q led

            N
         W   E
            S

           ♠ K 3
           ♡ A K Q J 10 9 8
           ◊ 3
           ♣ A 5 2

South	West	North	East
2♡	Pass	2♠	Pass
3♣	Pass	3◊	Pass
4 NT	Pass	5◊	Double
6♡	Pass	Pass	Pass

South's 2♡ opening was Acol, forcing for one round.

As his partner had doubled the Blackwood response of 5 ◊, West began with the ◊ Q, which was allowed to hold. West played a second diamond and South ruffed. Pleased that the opponents had not switched to a trump, South attempted to ruff the third club. To his dismay, he was overruffed.

"I think I played for the best chance," he said. "It was more likely that the clubs would stand up for three rounds than that the spades would be 3-3."

"I dare say," North replied. "But there were other points worth considering."

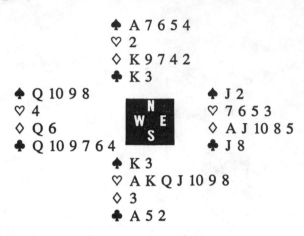

♠ A 7 6 5 4
♥ 2
♦ K 9 7 4 2
♣ K 3

♠ Q 10 9 8   ♠ J 2
♥ 4   ♥ 7 6 5 3
♦ Q 6   ♦ A J 10 8 5
♣ Q 10 9 7 6 4   ♣ J 8

♠ K 3
♥ A K Q J 10 9 8
♦ 3
♣ A 5 2

South played in 6♥ after East had doubled a Blackwood response of 5♦. West began with the ♦Q and followed with a second round. South ruffed and attempted to ruff the third round of clubs. He pointed out that a 6-2 break in clubs was less likely than a 4-2 break in spades.

North was not sympathetic. "That may be," he said, "but the fact that West had not played a trump at trick two was significant; it was quite likely that he knew you wouldn't be able to ruff a club. In addition to which, you had excellent squeeze chances. As the cards lie, this is the ending:

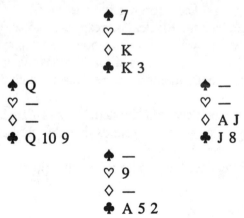

♠ 7
♥ —
♦ K
♣ K 3

♠ Q   ♠ —
♥ —   ♥ —
♦ —   ♦ A J
♣ Q 10 9   ♣ J 8

♠ —
♥ 9
♦ —
♣ A 5 2

"The last trump squeezes West. If East held three clubs there would be a double squeeze."

49 NOTHING TO SPARE

Dealer North
Both sides vulnerable

♠ A K 5 2
♡ Q J 7
◊ K Q 5 4
♣ J 2

♡2 led

```
      N
   W     E
      S
```

♠ 4 3
♡ A K 10 9 8 6
◊ 3 2
♣ 10 7 6

South	West	North	East
		1 ◊	1 NT
Double	2 ♠	Double	Pass
3 ♡	Pass	4 ♡	Pass
Pass	Pass		

South's double of 1 NT is very questionable. If partner is short of hearts and the declarer has a five-card minor, the result can easily be 'plus one.' It is better to bid a simple 2 ♡. North's double of 2 ♠ was also borderline.

Playing in 4 ♡, South won the trump lead and led a diamond to the queen and ace. East led a second trump, on which West showed out, and South finished a trick short, making just six hearts, two spades and one diamond.

"If a trump isn't led I can ruff a club," South remarked. "It had to be a singleton, too."

"As East bid 1 NT and was marked with a doubleton spade, the trumps were sure to be 3-1," North replied. "Also, you know that East has all the outstanding strength. You have to look for some other line of play."

Replay of 49

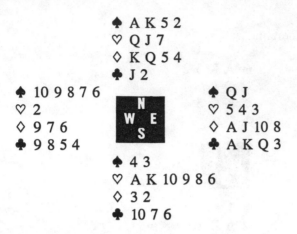

```
              ♠ A K 5 2
              ♡ Q J 7
              ◊ K Q 5 4
              ♣ J 2
  ♠ 10 9 8 7 6         ♠ Q J
  ♡ 2              N    ♡ 5 4 3
  ◊ 9 7 6      W   E    ◊ A J 10 8
  ♣ 9 8 5 4        S    ♣ A K Q 3
              ♠ 4 3
              ♡ A K 10 9 8 6
              ◊ 3 2
              ♣ 10 7 6
```

South played in 4 ♡ after East had overcalled with 1 NT and West had bid 2 ♠. West made the well judged lead of a trump. South led a diamond to the queen and ace, a trump was returned, and declarer was unable to find a tenth trick.

"You had a good picture of the distribution," North observed. "I think you should aim to bring pressure on East, who is marked with all the high cards. Suppose you begin with ace, king and another spade. East throws a club, and this leaves:

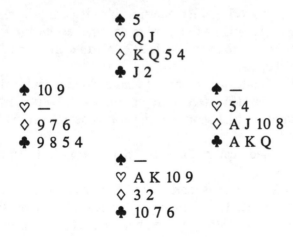

```
              ♠ 5
              ♡ Q J
              ◊ K Q 5 4
              ♣ J 2
  ♠ 10 9           ♠ —
  ♡ —              ♡ 5 4
  ◊ 9 7 6          ◊ A J 10 8
  ♣ 9 8 5 4        ♣ A K Q
              ♠ —
              ♡ A K 10 9
              ◊ 3 2
              ♣ 10 7 6
```

"Now you play a diamond to the queen. If East ducks, you play the fourth spade from dummy and East has no good discard. So let's say that East wins the diamond and returns a trump. Again, you lead dummy's fourth spade. What can East do? If he plays a trump you can eventually ruff the third club. And he can't spare either a diamond or a club."

50　AWKWARD MOMENT

Dealer South
Both sides vulnerable

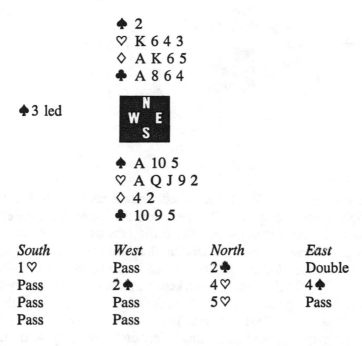

♠ 2
♡ K 6 4 3
◇ A K 6 5
♣ A 8 6 4

♠ 3 led

♠ A 10 5
♡ A Q J 9 2
◇ 4 2
♣ 10 9 5

South	West	North	East
1♡	Pass	2♣	Double
Pass	2♠	4♡	4♠
Pass	Pass	5♡	Pass
Pass	Pass		

North described his 2♣ response as 'tactical.' He wanted to find out more about his partner's hand, and there was the further point that he might avert a club lead.

South won the first spade, ruffed a spade, and returned to the ♡Q. East discarded on this trick and the contract was suddenly awkward. South ruffed the third spade, cashed the ♡K, and tried to return on the third round of diamonds. This was overruffed and he had to lose two clubs later.

"H'm," said North.

"What's that?"

"I just said h'm."

"You can h'm as much as you like. I can't make it."

"It was lay-down."

Replay of 50

```
              ♠ 2
              ♡ K 6 4 3
              ◊ A K 6 5
              ♣ A 8 6 4
 ♠ Q 7 6 3        N        ♠ K J 9 8 4
 ♡ 10 8 7 5    W     E     ♡ —
 ◊ 9 3            S        ◊ Q J 10 8 7
 ♣ 7 3 2                   ♣ K Q J
              ♠ A 10 5
              ♡ A Q J 9 2
              ◊ 4 2
              ♣ 10 9 5
```

South played in 5♡ after East had made a take-out double and strongly supported spades. Declarer won the spade lead, ruffed a spade, and crossed to the ♡ Q. After ruffing the last spade he cashed the ♡ K and tried to enter his hand on the third round of diamonds. This was overruffed and he still had to lose two club tricks.

"Funnily enough," South remarked. "I think I can make an over-trick if the trumps are 3-1. I play off four rounds, discarding clubs from dummy, and East is caught in a trump squeeze."

"That may be," said his partner, "but on the bidding the trumps were quite likely to be 4-0. I think the key play is to begin with the ♡ K from dummy. If East follows, you overtake, ruff the other spade, and make five at least. When East shows out on the ♡ K your best play is a low club. Say that East wins and returns a diamond. You duck another club and eventually discard a spade on the thirteenth club."

"That's double-dummy."

"Not really. East's most likely distribution is 5-0-5-3. Anyway, there's nothing else to play for when you see the trumps are 4-0."

51 SECOND CHOICE

Dealer North
Neither side vulnerable

♠ Q J 10
♡ —
♦ A K 8 6 4
♣ A Q J 8 7

♡ 8 led

```
    N
 W    E
    S
```

♠ A K 9 6 5
♡ Q 10 6 5
♦ J 2
♣ 6 5

South	West	North	East
		1 ♦	Pass
1 ♠	Pass	3 ♣	Pass
3 ♡	Double	3 ♠	Pass
5 ♣	Pass	6 ♣	Pass
Pass	Pass		

North's force on the second round was sure to include support for spades. This induced South to bid the fourth suit and then invite a slam.

West led a heart, which was ruffed in dummy. The declarer drew trumps in three rounds, discarding a diamond from the table, then finessed the ♣Q, which held the trick. He played ace, king and another diamond, but the suit was divided 4-2. So were the clubs, and South was left with two losing hearts at the finish.

"The entries were awkward," South remarked. "I wanted a 3-3 break in either clubs or diamonds."

"That's not how I would have looked at it," North replied.

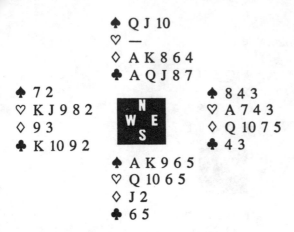

                    ♠ Q J 10
                    ♡ —
                    ◊ A K 8 6 4
                    ♣ A Q J 8 7

♠ 7 2   ♠ 8 4 3
♡ K J 9 8 2   ♡ A 7 4 3
◊ 9 3   ◊ Q 10 7 5
♣ K 10 9 2   ♣ 4 3

                    ♠ A K 9 6 5
                    ♡ Q 10 6 5
                    ◊ J 2
                    ♣ 6 5

Playing in 6♠, South ruffed the heart lead and drew trumps in three rounds, discarding a diamond from dummy. He finessed ♣Q and played off three rounds of diamonds. With neither diamonds nor clubs breaking, he finished a trick short.

"You had to assume that the club finesse would be right," said North, "so you have eleven tricks on top, by way of five spades, one ruff, two diamonds and three clubs. You didn't give yourself the chance of finding the diamonds 4-2. On the third trump discard a club from dummy, not a diamond. Then you can play ace, king and another diamond, followed by the club finesse. When this wins you can develop the twelfth trick in diamonds."

52 HIPPO DANCING

Dealer South
Both sides vulnerable

```
              ♠ 8 7 5 3
              ♡ Q 9 7
              ◊ K Q 4
              ♣ K 10 6
```

♠K led

```
        N
      W   E
        S
```

```
              ♠ A 6
              ♡ A K 6 4 2
              ◊ A 7 3
              ♣ A Q 5
```

South	West	North	East
1♣	Pass	1♡	Pass
2 NT	Pass	4 NT	Pass
5♡	Pass	5 NT	Pass
Pass	Pass		

North - South were playing the Blue Club in a big pairs event. North's 1♡ signified upwards of 6 points with fewer than three controls (two for an ace, one for a king). North should perhaps have bid 6♡ over 5♡. He did not expect his partner to subside in what Terence Reese once called the Hippopotamus contract of 5 NT.

West led the ♠K, which held the first trick, and followed with the jack. East played the 4 and the 10, and South formed the impression that the spades were 5-2. On the ♡A East dropped the 10. This could have been a false card from various combinations, so declarer played a second heart to dummy's queen. West turned up with four hearts and five spades, so the best that declarer could do was take ten tricks, for one down.

"That won't be too bad," said South. "Most people will be in 6♡."

"Some will, I agree," said North. "But I'm wondering whether you might have made 5 NT. I don't mean by finessing dummy's ♡9."

Replay of 52

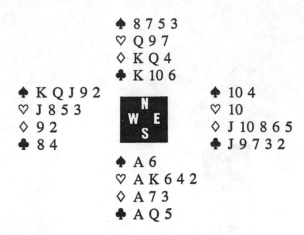

```
                    ♠ 8 7 5 3
                    ♡ Q 9 7
                    ◇ K Q 4
                    ♣ K 10 6
  ♠ K Q J 9 2          N           ♠ 10 4
  ♡ J 8 5 3        W       E       ♡ 10
  ◇ 9 2                S           ◇ J 10 8 6 5
  ♣ 8 4                             ♣ J 9 7 3 2
                    ♠ A 6
                    ♡ A K 6 4 2
                    ◇ A 7 3
                    ♣ A Q 5
```

Playing in an ungainly 5 NT, South won the second spade and played the ♡A, followed by a heart to the queen. When he found the suit 4-1 he had to take the ten top tricks.

"There wasn't any hurry to continue the hearts, was there?" North asked. "You retain more chances if you cash the minor suits first. After two spades, the ♡A, and five tricks in the minors the position is something like this:

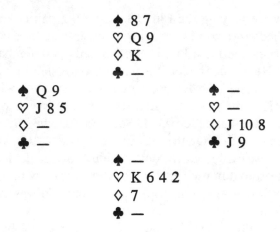

```
                    ♠ 8 7
                    ♡ Q 9
                    ◇ K
                    ♣ —
  ♠ Q 9                             ♠ —
  ♡ J 8 5                           ♡ —
  ◇ —                               ◇ J 10 8
  ♣ —                               ♣ J 9
                    ♠ —
                    ♡ K 6 4 2
                    ◇ 7
                    ♣ —
```

"You lead the ◇K and West has to throw a spade. You have a count of his hand now. A spade is led to the queen and you make the last trick rather neatly with the ♠7."

126

53 EARLY SURRENDER

Dealer North
North - South vulnerable

```
              ♠ A
              ♡ J 7 6
              ◇ A J 8 7
              ♣ A K 5 4 3
♡ A led
                  N
              W       E
                  S

              ♠ K Q J 10 9 8
              ♡ K
              ◇ 3 2
              ♣ 9 8 6 2
```

South	West	North	East
		1♣	Pass
1♠	Pass	2◇	Pass
3♠	Pass	4♠	Pass
Pass	Pass		

West began with the ♡ A and followed with a low heart. The jack was headed by the queen and South ruffed. He played a spade to the ace, came back with a heart ruff, and drew trumps. As the spades were 4-2, his trumps were now exhausted. When the clubs broke 3-1 he lost two more tricks in hearts.

"I can't do it with both suits breaking badly," South declared.

"I'm not so sure about that," North replied. "I don't think your timing was right."

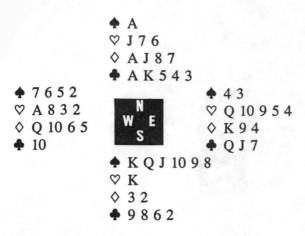

Playing in 4♠, South ruffed the second round of hearts, crossed to the ♠A, and returned to hand with a heart ruff. It took the rest of his trumps to draw West's, and when the clubs declined to break he was defeated.

"Does it help if instead of ruffing the second heart I throw a diamond?" South asked.

"No, it's not that," North replied. "They play a third heart and the position is the same. It's unusual play, but what happens if after the ♠A you lead the ♣A and a low club? You unblock, of course, keeping the 2. The position is then:

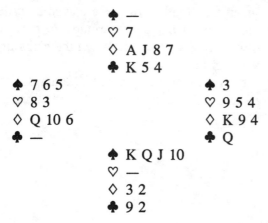

"The defenders have made two tricks, and all they can do now is take the club ruff."

54 HAPPY ENDING

Dealer West
Neither side vulnerable

```
                    ♠ A 10 8
                    ♡ Q 8
                    ◊ A K Q 9
                    ♣ J 9 3 2

♣K led              N
                  W   E
                    S

                    ♠ Q 4
                    ♡ A J 9 7 6 3
                    ◊ 4 2
                    ♣ 7 6 4
```

South	West	North	East
	1 ♠	1 NT	Pass
3 ♡	Pass	4 ♡	Pass
Pass	Pass		

North did well to raise the hearts rather than rebid 3 NT. He realized that there might be a lack of entries to the South hand.

The clubs were 3-3 and the defenders took the first three tricks. East switched to a spade and West's jack forced the ace from dummy. South took three rounds of diamonds, discarding his spade loser, then led the ♡Q, on which the 10 dropped from West. The jack was finessed on the next round, but East had begun with K x x x and had to make the king.

"I can't pick up the king of trumps," said South. "There weren't enough entries to dummy for any sort of trump coup."

North sighed and reached for the next board.

Replay of 54

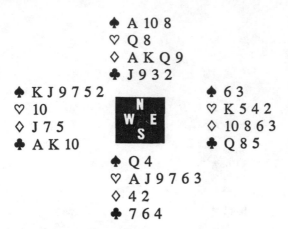

```
              ♠ A 10 8
              ♡ Q 8
              ◊ A K Q 9
              ♣ J 9 3 2
♠ K J 9 7 5 2                    ♠ 6 3
♡ 10                            ♡ K 5 4 2
◊ J 7 5                         ◊ 10 8 6 3
♣ A K 10                        ♣ Q 8 5
              ♠ Q 4
              ♡ A J 9 7 6 3
              ◊ 4 2
              ♣ 7 6 4
```

South played in 4 ♡ after West had opened the bidding. The defence began with three tricks in clubs, then East switched to a spade. South took a spade discard on the third diamond, then finessed the ♡ Q.

"It may not have been obvious," North conceded, "but I think you ought to test the hearts before cashing the three diamonds. It is true that this will cost a trick if the heart finesse is wrong, but in match play this won't matter. When the ♡ Q holds, you follow with the 8. Then you lead the thirteenth club from dummy. East discards a spade and so do you. The position is then:

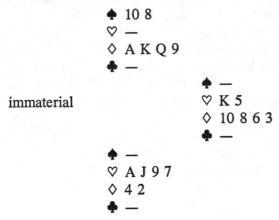

```
              ♠ 10 8
              ♡ —
              ◊ A K Q 9
              ♣ —
                               ♠ —
immaterial                     ♡ K 5
                               ◊ 10 8 6 3
                               ♣ —
              ♠ —
              ♡ A J 9 7
              ◊ 4 2
              ♣ —
```

"You ruff a spade, cross with a diamond, and ruff another spade. Now a diamond, and you are in dummy at trick twelve."

Dealer South
Both sides vulnerable

♠ Q J 8 7 5
♡ Q 9
◇ J 8 5
♣ 9 7 3

◇ 10 led

```
    N
 W     E
    S
```

♠ K 6 2
♡ A K
◇ A K Q
♣ A Q J 8 4

South	West	North	East
2♣	Pass	2◇	Pass
3 NT	Pass	4♡	Pass
4♠	Pass	4 NT	Pass
6 NT	Pass	Pass	Pass

North's 4♡ was a transfer to 4♠ and 4 NT was a slam suggestion. There was duplication, as it turned out, in both red suits.

West led a diamond against 6 NT and South began with the ♠K. West, who held A 9, held off and won the next round. There was only one entry to dummy now, and since East held K 10 x in clubs South had to go one down. He made just four spades, two hearts, three diamonds, and two clubs.

"Typical!" said South. "Mind you, I would have passed 3 NT on your hand. Perhaps I ought to have begun with a low spade instead of the king. That way, I can finesse twice in clubs."

"That seems to work better as the cards lie," said North cautiously.

```
                    ♠ Q J 8 7 5
                    ♡ Q 9
                    ◊ J 8 5
                    ♣ 9 7 3
     ♠ A 9                              ♠ 10 4 3
     ♡ J 8 6 4          N              ♡ 10 7 5 3 2
     ◊ 10 9 7 3 2    W     E           ◊ 6 4
     ♣ 6 2              S              ♣ K 10 5
                    ♠ K 6 2
                    ♡ A K
                    ◊ A K Q
                    ♣ A Q J 8 4
```

South played in 6 NT and West led the ◊ 10. The ♠K held the next trick. West won the second round and played another diamond. South obtained two discards on the long spades but was unable to pick up the ♣K.

Would a low spade to the queen have been a better play? A club finesse follows, then the ♠K loses to the ace, and there is an entry for a second finesse in clubs.

But there is another point, which escaped the notice even of the omniscient North. With A x of spades West, on lead of the 2, must play the ace! Then the declarer cannot obtain the entries required for two club finesses.

Assuming best defence, the only time when it helps to begin with the king is when either East or West holds a singleton ace. You make fewer spade tricks, but you can finesse twice in clubs.

So, what is the best play? In a perfect world, the spade king; but since few defenders would play the ace from A x in the West position, the best tactical play may be to begin with a low spade.

56 JACK IN THE BOX

Dealer South
Both sides vulnerable

```
              ♠ 10 9 3
              ♡ J 7 5 4
              ◇ A Q J
              ♣ A 3 2

   ♡ 10 led        N
               W       E
                   S

              ♠ A K Q J 8
              ♡ A
              ◇ 10 9 3 2
              ♣ 10 7 4
```

South	West	North	East
1♠	Pass	2♣	Pass
2◇	Pass	3♠	Pass
4♠	Pass	Pass	Pass

Modern bidding!

West led the ♡ 10 to South's ace. On the second round of trumps East discarded a diamond. There seemed no reason to leave trumps at large, so the declarer drew two more rounds, discarding a club from dummy, while East threw another diamond and a club. South followed with ace and queen of diamonds. East won and led a low heart in this position:

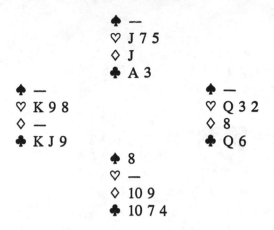

```
                    ♠ —
                    ♡ J 7 5
                    ◇ J
                    ♣ A 3
  ♠ —                                ♠ —
  ♡ K 9 8                            ♡ Q 3 2
  ◇ —                                ◇ 8
  ♣ K J 9                            ♣ Q 6
                    ♠ 8
                    ♡ —
                    ◇ 10 9
                    ♣ 10 7 4
```

South discarded two clubs on the hearts, but he had to ruff the fourth round. Then the diamonds were blocked.

"I suppose I ought to have made it somehow," said South.

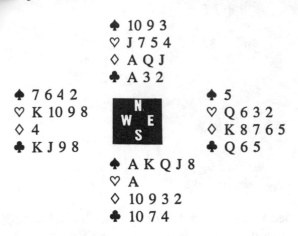

♠ 10 9 3
♡ J 7 5 4
◊ A Q J
♣ A 3 2

♠ 7 6 4 2
♡ K 10 9 8
◊ 4
♣ K J 9 8

♠ 5
♡ Q 6 3 2
◊ K 8 7 6 5
♣ Q 6 5

♠ A K Q J 8
♡ A
◊ 10 9 3 2
♣ 10 7 4

West led the ♡ 10 against 4 ♠. South drew four rounds of trumps; dummy discarded a club, East two diamonds and a club. After ace and queen of diamonds the defenders played on hearts. South had to ruff the fourth round with his last trump. Now the diamonds were blocked and South lost a club at the finish.

"Perhaps I should have thrown the ◊ J earlier," South suggested.

"Then East can let the ace and queen hold," North replied. "The awkward card was dummy's fourth heart. Suppose you throw a heart from dummy on the fourth spade. You reach this position:

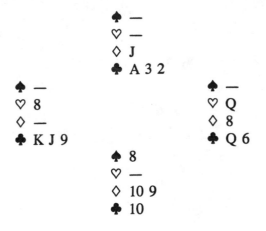

♠ —
♡ —
◊ J
♣ A 3 2

♠ —
♡ 8
◊ —
♣ K J 9

♠ —
♡ Q
◊ 8
♣ Q 6

♠ 8
♡ —
◊ 10 9
♣ 10

"Now, when they play a fourth heart, you can dispose of the ◊ J."

57 JAWS

Dealer South
East - West vulnerable

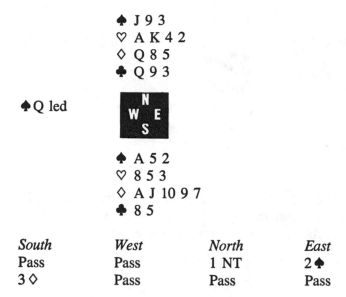

♠ J 9 3
♡ A K 4 2
◊ Q 8 5
♣ Q 9 3

♠ Q led

N
W   E
S

♠ A 5 2
♡ 8 5 3
◊ A J 10 9 7
♣ 8 5

South	West	North	East
Pass	Pass	1 NT	2♠
3 ◊	Pass	Pass	Pass

As North - South were playing a weak notrump and South had passed originally, South's 3 ◊ bid was not forcing.

West's lead of the ♠ Q, presumably a singleton, ran to the ace. South led a heart to dummy, noting the fall of the 10 from East. The ◊ 8 was covered by a singleton king and trumps were drawn in four rounds, East discarded two spades and one club, dummy a heart.

East appeared to hold 6-2-1-4 distribution, and it occurred to South that if he could duck a round of hearts to East's jack or 9, East would be forced to concede a trick to the dummy, either in spades or clubs. This plan failed because West, who held Q 9 7 6 of hearts, went up with the queen — the Crocodile coup. It was then impossible to endplay East.

"You see what I was playing for?" said South. "Some people write too many books," he added darkly.

"You shouldn't have given him the chance," said North.

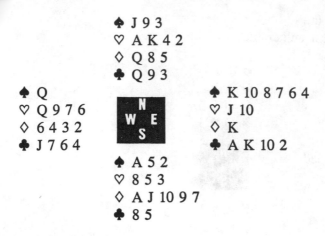

♠ J 9 3
♡ A K 4 2
◊ Q 8 5
♣ Q 9 3

♠ Q
♡ Q 9 7 6
◊ 6 4 3 2
♣ J 7 6 4

♠ K 10 8 7 6 4
♡ J 10
◊ K
♣ A K 10 2

♠ A 5 2
♡ 8 5 3
◊ A J 10 9 7
♣ 8 5

South played in 3 ◊ after East had overcalled in spades. He won the spade lead and played a heart to the ace, noting the fall of East's 10. After four rounds of diamonds the position was:

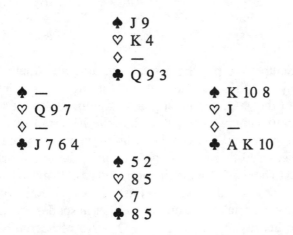

♠ J 9
♡ K 4
◊ —
♣ Q 9 3

♠ —
♡ Q 9 7
◊ —
♣ J 7 6 4

♠ K 10 8
♡ J
◊ —
♣ A K 10

♠ 5 2
♡ 8 5
◊ 7
♣ 8 5

Now South led a heart, intending to duck the trick to East, but West defeated this play by going up with the ♡Q.

"You should have led your last diamond, discarding another heart from dummy," said North. "Say that East throws another spade. Then you cross to the king of hearts and exit with a spade, making the ninth trick with the ♣Q."

58 CUT AND RUN

Dealer South
Neither side vulnerable

```
              ♠ 3 2
              ♡ Q 4 2
              ◇ Q 7 6
              ♣ 10 9 7 5 4

♡9 led        N
           W  E
              S

              ♠ A Q J 8 7 5
              ♡ A K
              ◇ J 10 9 5
              ♣ 2
```

South	West	North	East
1♠	Pass	Pass	1 NT
2♠	Pass	Pass	Pass

West's lead of the ♡9 ran to the king. South cashed the ♡A, then led the ◇10. East, who held A x, won with the ace and returned a diamond to West's king. A diamond ruff followed. West then came in with a club and a fourth diamond was ruffed. When South ruffed the next club and played ace and queen of spades, he found the king still guarded. Thus he was one down, having lost two diamonds, a club, two ruffs, and the ♠K.

"Was it necessary to lose *all* those tricks?" North demanded.

"I couldn't help it. I had to get a diamond trick going; otherwise, with the spades 4-1, I lose a spade to the king, ace and king of diamonds, two ruffs and a club."

"That's just what you did lose. You can save one of those tricks, surely."

```
                    ♠ 3 2
                    ♡ Q 4 2
                    ◊ Q 7 6
                    ♣ 10 9 7 5 4
   ♠ 6                              ♠ K 10 9 4
   ♡ 9 8 7 5         N              ♡ J 10 6 3
   ◊ K 8 3 2       W   E            ◊ A 4
   ♣ A Q 6 3         S              ♣ K J 8
                    ♠ A Q J 8 7 5
                    ♡ A K
                    ◊ J 10 9 5
                    ♣ 2
```

South played in 2 ♠ and West led the ♡ 9. South cashed the second heart, then led a diamond. The defence took two diamonds, a diamond ruff, a club and another ruff. East still made the ♠ K, for one down.

"You mustn't let West get in twice to give his partner two ruffs," North pointed out. "Cash the second heart if you like, then lead your singleton club. It's a form of *Scissors Coup*. East gets only one diamond ruff. You hold the defence to a club, two diamonds, a ruff, and the ♠ K."

Dealer South
Both sides vulnerable

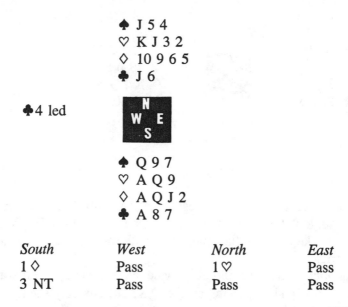

♠ J 5 4
♡ K J 3 2
◊ 10 9 6 5
♣ J 6

♣4 led

♠ Q 9 7
♡ A Q 9
◊ A Q J 2
♣ A 8 7

South	West	North	East
1 ◊	Pass	1 ♡	Pass
3 NT	Pass	Pass	Pass

West led the ♣4. South tried the jack from dummy, but East covered with the queen and returned the 10. West overtook and played a third round, on which dummy discarded a diamond and East a low spade.

South played off four rounds of hearts, the suit breaking 3-3. On the fourth round everyone discarded a spade. The first diamond finesse held, but the suit broke 4-1 and South was unable to develop a ninth trick.

Entering 100 to the opposition, South noted that his partner was looking thoughtful. "I know I could have done it if I had overtaken the ♡Q and then the 9," he said, "but the hearts were more likely to be 4-2 than the diamonds 4-1."

"That's true," North replied. "I was thinking of something else."

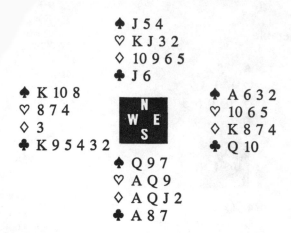

```
              ♠ J 5 4
              ♡ K J 3 2
              ◇ 10 9 6 5
              ♣ J 6
♠ K 10 8                        ♠ A 6 3 2
♡ 8 7 4          N             ♡ 10 6 5
◇ 3          W       E         ◇ K 8 7 4
♣ K 9 5 4 3 2    S             ♣ Q 10
              ♠ Q 9 7
              ♡ A Q 9
              ◇ A Q J 2
              ♣ A 8 7
```

South played in 3 NT and West led a low club. South won the third round, took four rounds of hearts, then ran the ◇ 10. This held, but East had kept all his diamonds and South was unable to develop a ninth trick.

South noticed that he could have made the contract by overtaking twice in hearts and so picking up the ◇ K, but this play seemed to be against the odds.

"You want to know how the hearts break," his partner remarked. "Suppose you begin with the *queen* of hearts. West will surely signal his length, to tell his partner how long to hold up. When West plays the 4 it becomes reasonably safe to overtake and run the ◇ 10. It's true that the ♡4 *might* be a singleton; but a singleton diamond in the West hand is more likely than a singleton heart."

South
~~i~~ - South vulnerable

♠ K J 9 5
♡ Q 4 3 2
◇ 8 7
♣ A 3 2

♠ 2 led

```
  N
W   E
  S
```

♠ Q 10 8 4
♡ K 6
◇ A J 9 4
♣ K 10 8

South	West	North	East
1 ◇	Pass	1 ♡	Pass
1 ♠	Pass	3 ♠	Pass
Pass	Pass		

South's rebid of 1 ♠, in preference to 1 NT, does not commend itself to either of the present authors.

West led a low trump. South won in dummy and ran the ◇ 8 to West's 10. West then played ace and another spade. East discarded a club. A heart went to the king and ace, and West returned the jack to dummy's queen. After a heart ruff, ◇ A and a diamond ruff, South was down to:

```
        ♠ —
        ♡ 4
        ◇ —
        ♣ A 3 2

        ♠ —
        ♡ —
        ◇ J
        ♣ K 10 8
```

South made only two more tricks and finished one down. "It's
easy if they don't lead a trump," he remarked.

"You gave up too soon," his partner replied.

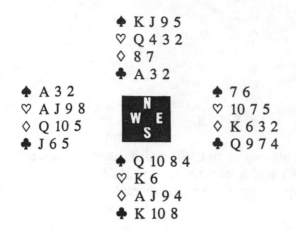

```
              ♠ K J 9 5
              ♡ Q 4 3 2
              ◊ 8 7
              ♣ A 3 2
♠ A 3 2                        ♠ 7 6
♡ A J 9 8         N            ♡ 10 7 5
◊ Q 10 5      W       E        ◊ K 6 3 2
♣ J 6 5           S            ♣ Q 9 7 4
              ♠ Q 10 8 4
              ♡ K 6
              ◊ A J 9 4
              ♣ K 10 8
```

West led a low trump against 3♠. When South let the ◊8 run to the 10, West played ace and another spade. The ♡K lost to the ace and the jack was returned. South played ace and another diamond, then ruffed a heart, arriving at this position:

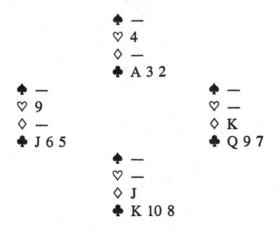

```
              ♠ —
              ♡ 4
              ◊ —
              ♣ A 3 2
♠ —                           ♠ —
♡ 9                           ♡ —
◊ —                           ◊ K
♣ J 6 5                       ♣ Q 9 7
              ♠ —
              ♡ —
              ◊ J
              ♣ K 10 8
```

South played a club to the ace, then conceded one down.

"Instead of leading a club, try the ◊J," North suggested. "West has to throw a club, you discard the heart from dummy, and East wins. East's best chance now is the ♣Q, but you should get it right. It's an unusual ending."

Dealer West
Neither side vulnerable

```
                    ♠ K Q 8 6 2
                    ♡ 9 6 3 2
                    ◇ K J 6
                    ♣ 3
    ♡ A led        ┌─────────┐
                   │    N    │
                   │ W     E │
                   │    S    │
                   └─────────┘
                    ♠ A J 10 7 3
                    ♡ —
                    ◇ 10 9 7 5 2
                    ♣ Q J 9
```

South	West	North	East
	Pass	Pass	1 ♡
1 ♠	3 ♡	4 ♠	Pass
Pass	Pass		

South ruffed the heart lead and drew trumps in two rounds, East discarding a heart. A diamond went to the jack and ace, and East led another heart, which South ruffed. Declarer now ran the ◇ 10, but East produced the queen and led a third heart. This took South's last trump and he was left with two losers in dummy, a heart and a club.

"I knew East's ◇ A might be a false card," said South, who evidently had not considered this possibility, "but I had to allow for West holding Q x x x."

"Were you trying to make the contract or to make overtricks?" North inquired.

```
              ♠ K Q 8 6 2
              ♡ 9 6 3 2
              ◊ K J 6
              ♣ 3
♠ 9 4                          ♠ 5
♡ A J 7 4         N            ♡ K Q 10 8 5
◊ 8 3          W     E         ◊ A Q 4
♣ K 8 6 5 4       S            ♣ A 10 7 2
              ♠ A J 10 7 3
              ♡ —
              ◊ 10 9 7 5 2
              ♣ Q J 9
```

South played in 4♠ after East had opened 1♡ and West had raised to 3♡. South ruffed the heart lead, drew trumps in two rounds, and led a diamond to the jack, which East won with the ace. East returned a heart, South ruffed and ran the ◊ 10. This lost to the queen and the next heart forced the declarer's last trump. The diamonds were blocked and dummy was left with a losing heart and a losing club.

"That was an interesting exercise in how to convert ten tricks into nine," said North. "The most you can lose, if you don't block the diamonds, is two diamonds and a club. On the second round go up with the king and clear the suit while you still have a trump in your hand."

Dealer East
Neither side vulnerable

```
                       ♠ 8 5 4 2
                       ♡ K 7 2
                       ◊ Q 10 9
                       ♣ A K 3

    ♠ 6 led            ┌─────────┐
                       │   N     │
                       │ W   E   │
                       │   S     │
                       └─────────┘

                       ♠ —
                       ♡ A J 4
                       ◊ A K J 6 3
                       ♣ J 8 7 6 5
```

South	West	North	East
			2♠
Double	3♠	4♠	Double
5◊	Pass	6◊	Pass
Pass	Pass		

East's double of 4♠ was of a type often made by moderate players. It achieved nothing and considerably extended South's options. He could pass, redouble, or bid freely, and on this occasion it enabled him to show without any risk that he had a promising hand. If North bid 5♡ over 5◊, he could show his second suit, knowing that there must be a fit.

A low spade went to the ace and South ruffed. He drew trumps in three rounds and played off ace and king of clubs. West won the next club and exited with a spade. Now South needed the heart finesse, and this was wrong, too.

"We were in a good contract," said South. "I wanted the ♣Q to fall or the heart finesse."

"It was quite likely that West would hold both queens," North replied. "You could have managed it better."

```
              ♠ 8 5 4 2
              ♡ K 7 2
              ◇ Q 10 9
              ♣ A K 3
♠ Q 9 6                        ♠ A K J 10 7 3
♡ Q 10 8 5       N             ♡ 9 6 3
◇ 8 7 2        W   E           ◇ 5 4
♣ Q 10 4         S             ♣ 9 2
              ♠ —
              ♡ A J 4
              ◇ A K J 6 3
              ♣ J 8 7 6 5
```

South played in 6◇ after East had opened with a weak 2♠ and West had offered support. South ruffed the spade lead, drew trumps, and played three rounds of clubs, losing to the queen. West exited with a spade and later made the ♡Q, for one down.

"The general plan," said North, "should have been to ruff three spades and knock out the ♣Q while you still have a trump in hand. After ruffing the spade lead play a club to the ace, ruff a spade, cross to the ♣K, ruff a third spade high and concede a club. You still have a high trump and everything is under control."

63 A CHANCE TO IMPRESS

Dealer South
Neither side vulnerable

```
              ♠ J 8 7 2
              ♡ Q 7 6 3
              ◇ 8 4
              ♣ A 3 2

   ♠ 5 led        N
                W   E
                  S

              ♠ —
              ♡ K J 9 8 4
              ◇ A J 7
              ♣ K Q 10 8 7
```

South	West	North	East
1♡	Pass	2♡	2♠
4♡	4♠	5♡	Pass
Pass	Double	Pass	Pass
Pass			

West began with a low spade and South ruffed. When the ♡J was led, West gave it a small look, then played low. South led another heart, and now West went up with the ace and played a third round. The clubs broke 4-1, so declarer had to ruff the fourth round with dummy's last trump. He was left with two losing diamonds and finished one down.

"I thought I was going to make it," said South. "If the clubs had broken 3-2 I would have done."

"You did notice West's slight hesitation on the first heart?" asked North.

"Yes, I suppose so. But it doesn't make any difference."

"Are you sure? I think it marked West with A 10 x. You have a good chance to make 5♡ if you draw that inference."

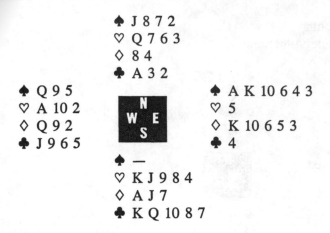

```
            ♠ J 8 7 2
            ♡ Q 7 6 3
            ◊ 8 4
            ♣ A 3 2
♠ Q 9 5                      ♠ A K 10 6 4 3
♡ A 10 2         N           ♡ 5
◊ Q 9 2       W   E          ◊ K 10 6 5 3
♣ J 9 6 5        S           ♣ 4
            ♠ —
            ♡ K J 9 8 4
            ◊ A J 7
            ♣ K Q 10 8 7
```

North - South had the better of the auction, playing in 5♡ doubled. East - West would have had a good chance in 5♠.

South ruffed the spade lead and played the ♡J, which was allowed to hold. West won the next trump and played a third round. Now dummy's remaining heart was needed for a ruff of the fourth club, and South finished one down.

West had hesitated for a moment before playing low on the first round of hearts, and there were in any case good grounds for placing him with three trumps. "When the ♡J held you should have played on clubs," North declared. "♣K, club to the ace, spade ruff, ♣Q, ruff the fourth club and ruff another spade. That brings you to:

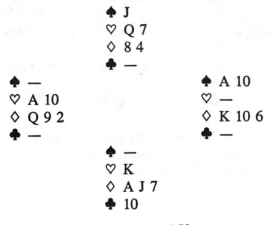

```
            ♠ J
            ♡ Q 7
            ◊ 8 4
            ♣ —
♠ —                         ♠ A 10
♡ A 10                      ♡ —
◊ Q 9 2                     ◊ K 10 6
♣ —                         ♣ —
            ♠ —
            ♡ K
            ◊ A J 7
            ♣ 10
```

152

"You haven't lost a trick yet, remember. Lead the fifth d
ruffs, you overruff and lead the last spade from dummy. I.
neat."

Dealer South
Neither side vulnerable

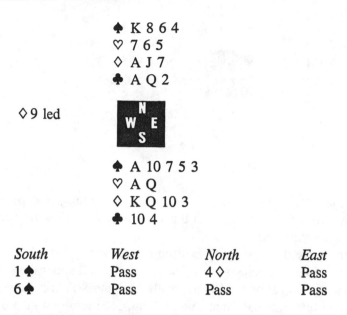

♠ K 8 6 4
♡ 7 6 5
◇ A J 7
♣ A Q 2

◇ 9 led

N
W E
S

♠ A 10 7 5 3
♡ A Q
◇ K Q 10 3
♣ 10 4

South	West	North	East
1 ♠	Pass	4 ◇	Pass
6 ♠	Pass	Pass	Pass

North's 4 ◇ showed the values for a good raise to game. South decided that he had enough to go for a slam and that there was no point in showing where his controls lay.

South won the diamond lead in dummy and advanced the ♠ K, on which West dropped the jack. After some thought South finessed the ♠ 10, which lost to the queen. Now he needed two finesses, and the club finesse was wrong.

"I think I played the trumps the right way," South remarked. "With Q J West might have played the queen on the first round — isn't that the argument?"

"Yes," said North, "but there was another line that would have given you an extra chance."

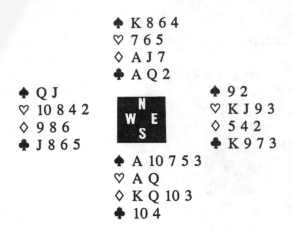

♠ K 8 6 4
♡ 7 6 5
◇ A J 7
♣ A Q 2

♠ Q J
♡ 10 8 4 2
◇ 9 8 6
♣ J 8 6 5

♠ 9 2
♡ K J 9 3
◇ 5 4 2
♣ K 9 7 3

♠ A 10 7 5 3
♡ A Q
◇ K Q 10 3
♣ 10 4

West led the ◇9 against 6♠. South won in dummy and played the ♠K, followed by a spade to the 10, which lost. Now he could not avoid a club loser.

"I don't say that your play in trumps was wrong," said North, "but it would have been good play, when the ♠J fell under the king, to finesse the ♡Q at once. When it holds, cash the ♡A and the ♠A. If you find that East has three trumps, return to dummy with a diamond, ruff the third heart, and then play on diamonds. This way, you win whether trumps are 2-2 or 3-1."

South gave this some thought, then raised an objection: "West might have played the ♠J from Q J 9. If I find that he has the trump winner, the first finesse must be in clubs, not in hearts."

"That's true, said North, a little surprised. "As a declarer you are quite a good defender."

Dealer South
North - South vulnerable

          ♠ 10 9 7 6 4
          ♡ Q 10 9
          ◇ K J 9 8
          ♣ 7

♠K led

```
  N
W   E
  S
```

♠ A 8
♡ A K 8 6 5 2
◇ A Q 6
♣ A J

South	West	North	East
2♣	Double	Pass	4♣
4♡	Pass	5◇	Pass
5♠	Pass	6♣	Pass
7♡	Pass	Pass	Pass

This was good bidding by North - South. When North, after passing on the first round, bid 5◇ over 4♡, it was certain that he was moving towards a slam in hearts. South's 5♠ was a grand slam try and North's 6♣ promised second round control of this suit.

(Although the point is seldom raised, there are good grounds, after the double of 2♣, for allowing opener's partner to respond at once on moderate hands. Then his side is less likely to be shut out by a jump in clubs.)

West led the ♠K against the grand slam. South won and laid down the ♡A. West showed out and it was then impossible for the declarer to ruff his second club and pick up the trumps without loss.

"That sort of thing can only happen to me," South grumbled.

"Only you could play it that way," said North unkindly.

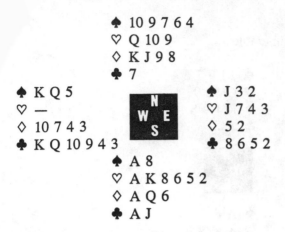

```
                 ♠ 10 9 7 6 4
                 ♡ Q 10 9
                 ◊ K J 9 8
                 ♣ 7
♠ K Q 5                              ♠ J 3 2
♡ —                                 ♡ J 7 4 3
◊ 10 7 4 3                           ◊ 5 2
♣ K Q 10 9 4 3                       ♣ 8 6 5 2
                 ♠ A 8
                 ♡ A K 8 6 5 2
                 ◊ A Q 6
                 ♣ A J
```

North - South did well to reach 7♡ after West had doubled the opening 2♣. South won the first trick with the ♠A and led the ♡A. When West showed out, South was a trick short. He could still pick up East's trumps and discard a spade on the long diamond, but he remained with a losing club.

"Your trumps were good enough to pick up J x x x on either side," North pointed out, "but you couldn't ruff a club and pick up four trumps in the West hand. The hand plays quite easily if you begin with a low heart to the queen. You return the 10, which East may cover; then you take the club ruff, pick up East's two hearts, and discard the spade loser on the long diamond."

1986 Publications

Kelsey, H. W.
COUNTDOWN TO BETTER BRIDGE

This book teaches the reader how to count the distribution and high cards in the hidden hands — the secret to all expert declarer play and defense. It is designed to sharpen your perception of what is occurring at the table, by getting you in the habit of correct patterns of thought. Recommended for: intermediate to expert.   Paperback $9.95

Reese, Terence, and Hoffman, Martin
PLAY IT AGAIN, SAM

65 interesting hands that were handled in the way most reasonable players would tackle them; then the best line of play is discussed. These are presented as problems, so you can work at each hand and decide what was wrong with the declarer's plan.
Paperback $7.95

THE CHAMPIONSHIP BRIDGE
Volume III
No. 25 Popular Systems I by A. Bernstein R. Baron
No. 26 Popular Systems II by A. Bernstein ar R. Baron
No. 27 Lebensohl by Eric Rodwell
No. 28 New Minor Forcing & Fourth Suit Forcing ar. Artificial by Jeff Meckstroth
No. 29 Minor Suit Raises by Marty Bergen
No. 30 Sacrifices by Bobby Wolff
No. 31 Is It Forcing? by Jim Jacoby
No. 32 2♣ — Strong, Artificial and Forcing by Mary Jane Farell
No. 33 Slam Bidding by Dr. G. Rosenkranz
No. 34 Counting by Ron Andersen
No. 35 Squeeze Play by Robert Hamman
No. 36 Modern Defensive Signals by K. Woolsey

In-depth discussions of the most widely used conventions . . . how to play them, when to use them and how to defend against them. The solution for those costly partnership misunderstandings. Written by some of the world's top experts.   95¢ each

95¢ each
12 for $9.95

THE BEST OF DEVYN PRESS
Newly Published Bridge Books

..NING BRIDGE INTANGIBLES
by Mike Lawrence and Keith Hanson $2.95

..s book shows you how to achieve the best results possible with the knowledge you already possess. ..iew of the topics covered are: how to be a good partner, how to avoid giving the opponents crucial ..formation, how to develop the best attitude at the table, and the best way to form a partnership. ..Recommended for: beginner through advanced.

THE FLANNERY TWO-DIAMOND CONVENTION
by Bill Flannery $7.95

Finally, a complete book on the Flannery convention, written by its creator. This teaches you the secrets to success so you will never have a misunderstanding with your partner. Included are sections on the mechanics, defenses against Flannery, the correct opening lead against the opponents' auctions, 62 example hands with explanations, and much more. Recommended for: intermediate through expert.

BRIDGE: THE BIDDER'S GAME
by Dr. George Rosenkranz $12.95

Bidding for the 80's; the concepts top experts are using today to increase their slam, game, part score, and competitive accuracy. Included are: an introduction to relays and how they can be incorporated into your present system, trump-asking and control-asking bids, new methods of cue bidding, revisions of popular conventions such as Stayman and Splinter bids, a complete update of the Romex System, with hundreds of examples. Recommended for: advanced through expert.

HAVE I GOT A STORY FOR YOU
by Patty Eber and Mike Freeman $7.95

These are humorous stories on bridge, submitted by players across the country, from the local to national level. Hundreds contributed their favorite tales; these are the best from club games, tournaments, bars and hospitality rooms. This entertaining collection is a perfect gift and is recommended for: anyone who enjoys bridge.

THE ART OF LOGICAL BIDDING
by Andrew Gorski $4.95

If you're tired of memorizing bidding sequences and still getting mediocre results at the table, this book is for you. It presents a new system, based on the inherent logic of the game. Because of the natural approach it reduces the chances of partnership misunderstandings, so you'll feel confident of reaching the best contract. Recommended for: bright beginner through intermediate.

STANDARD PLAYS OF CARD COMBINATIONS FOR
CONTRACT BRIDGE by Alan Truscott,
Laura Jane Gordy, and Edward L. Gordy $6.95

Contains the 150 most important card combinations so that you can maximize your trick-taking potential. The one skill that all experts possess is the ability to handle the standard plays correctly; here is this crucial information at your fingertips. Included are plays to the opening lead, suit-handling and finesses, second hand play and third hand play. Perforated so you may remove the cards from the book if you wish. Recommended for: beginner through advanced.

THE BEST OF DEVYN PRESS

Bridge Conventions Complete
by Amalya Kearse
$17.95

An undated and expanded edition (over 800 pages) of the reference book no duplicate player can afford to be without. The reviews say it all:

"At last! A book with both use and appeal for expert or novice plus everybody in between. Every partnership will find material they will wish to add to their present system. Not only are all the conventions in use anywhere today clearly and aptly described, but Kearse criticizes various treatments regarding potential flaws and how they can be circumvented.

"Do yourself a favor and add this book to your shelf even if you don't enjoy most bridge books. This book is a treat as well as a classic."
—ACBL BULLETIN

"A must for duplicate fans, this is a comprehensive, well-written guide through the maze of systems and conventions. This should be particularly useful to those who don't want to be taken off guard by an unfamiliar convention, because previously it would have been necessary to amass several references to obtain all the information presented."
—BRIDGE WORLD MAGAZINE

Published January, 1984

Recommended for: all duplicate players

ISBN 0-910791-07-4 paperback

Test Your Play As Declarer, Volume 1
by Jeff Rubens and Paul Lukacs
$5.95

Any reader who studies this book carefully will certainly become much more adept at playing out a hand. There are 89 hands here, each emphasizing a particular point in declarer play. The solution to each problem explains how and why a declarer should handle his hands in a certain way. A reprint of the original.

Published December, 1983

Recommended for: intermediate through expert

ISBN 0-910791-12-0 paperback

Devyn Press Book of Partnership Understanding
by Mike Lawrence
$2.95

Stop bidding misunderstandings before they occur with this valuable guide. It covers all the significant points you should discuss with your partner, whether you are forming a new partnership or you have played together for years.

Published December, 1983

Recommended for: novice through expert

ISBN 0-910791-08-2 paperback

101 Bridge Maxims
by H. W. Kelsey
$7.95

The experience of a master player and writer condensed into 101 easy-to-understand adages. Each hand will help you remember these essential rules during the heat of battle.

Published December, 1983

Recommended for: bright beginner through advanced.

ISBN 0-910791-10-4 paperback

Play Bridge with Mike Lawrence
by Mike Lawrence
$9.95

Follow Mike through a 2-session matchpoint event at a regional tournament, and learn how to gather information from the auction, the play of the cards and the atmosphere at the table. When to go against the field, compete, make close doubles, and more.

Published December, 1983

Recommended for: bright beginner through expert.

ISBN 0-910791-09-0 paperback

Play These Hands With Me
by Terence Reese
$7.95

Studies 60 hands in minute detail. How to analyze your position and sum up information you have available, with a post-mortem reviewing main points.

Published December, 1983

Recommended for: intermediate through expert.

ISBN 0-910791-11-2 paperback

THE BEST OF DEVYN PRESS
Bridge Books

MATCHPOINTS
by Kit Woolsey
$9.95

The long-awaited second book by the author of the classic *Partnership Defense*. *Matchpoints* examines all of the crucial aspects of duplicate bridge. It is surprising, with the wealth of excellent books on bidding and play, how neglected matchpoint strategy has been—Kit has filled that gap forever with the best book ever written on the subject. The chapters include: general concepts, constructive bidding, competitive bidding, defensive bidding and the play.
Published October, 1982
Recommended for: intermediate through expert.
ISBN 0-910791-00-7 paperback

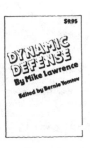

DYNAMIC DEFENSE
by Mike Lawrence
$9.95

One of the top authors of the '80's has produced a superior work in his latest effort. These unique hands offer you an over-the-shoulder look at how a World Champion reasons through the most difficult part of bridge. You will improve your technique as you sit at the table and attempt to find the winning sequence of plays. Each of the 65 problems is thoroughly explained and analyzed in the peerless Lawrence style.
Published October, 1982.
Recommended for: bright beginner through expert.
ISBN 0-910791-01-5 paperback

MODERN IDEAS IN BIDDING
by Dr. George Rosenkranz and Alan Truscott
$9.95

Mexico's top player combines with the bridge editor of the New York Times to produce a winner's guide to bidding theory. Constructive bidding, slams, pre-emptive bidding, competitive problems, overcalls and many other valuable concepts are covered in depth. Increase your accuracy with the proven methods which have won numerous National titles and have been adopted by a diverse group of champions.
Published October, 1982
Recommended for: intermediate through expert.
ISBN 0-910791-02-3 paperback

THE COMPLETE BOOK OF OPENING LEADS
by Easley Blackwood
$12.95

An impressive combination: the most famous name in bridge has compiled the most comprehensive book ever written on opening leads. Almost every situation imaginable is presented with a wealth of examples from world championship play. Learn to turn your wild guesses into intelligent thrusts at the enemy declarer by using all the available information. Chapters include when to lead long suits, dangerous opening leads, leads against slam contracts, doubling for a lead, when to lead partner's suit, and many others.
Published November, 1982.
Recommended for: beginner through advanced.
ISBN 0-910791-05-8 paperback

THE BEST OF DEVYN PRESS ❧

$4.95

The Devyn Press Book of BRIDGE PUZZLES By Alfred Sheinwold

Number 1

DEVYN PRESS BOOK OF BRIDGE PUZZLES #1, #2, and #3
by Alfred Sheinwold
$4.95 each

Each of the three books in this series is part of the most popular and entertaining collection of bridge problems ever written. They were originally titled "Pocket Books of Bridge Puzzles #1, #2, and #3." The 90 hands in each volume are practical and enjoyable—the kind that you attempt to solve every time you play. They also make perfect gifts for your friends, whether they are inexperienced novices or skilled masters.
Published January, 1981. Paperback
Recommended for: beginner through advanced.

TICKETS TO THE DEVIL
by Richard Powell $5.95

This is the most popular bridge novel ever written by the author of Woody Allen's "Bananas," "The Young Philadelphians," and Elvis Presley's "Follow That Dream."

Tickets has a cast of characters ranging from the Kings and Queens of tournament bridge down to the deuces. Among them are:

Ace McKinley, famous bridge columnist who needs a big win to restore his fading reputation.

Carole Clark, who lost a husband because she led a singleton king.

Bubba Worthington, young socialite who seeks the rank of Life Master to prove his virility.

The Dukes and the Ashcrafts, who have partnership troubles in bridge and in bed.

Tony Manuto, who plays for pay, and handles cards as if they were knives.

Powell shuffles these and many other players to deal out comedy, violence and drama in a perfect mixture.

TICKETS TO THE DEVIL $5.95

D ♠

A Novel by RICHARD POWELL
Introduction by RICHARD FREY

Published 1979. . .Paperback
Recommended for: all bridge players.

PARTNERSHIP DEFENSE
by Kit Woolsey
$8.95

Kit's first book is unanimously considered THE classic defensive text so that you can learn the secrets of the experts. It contains a detailed discussion of attitude, count, and suit-preference signals; leads; matchpoints; defensive conventions; protecting partner; with quizzes and a unique partnership test at the end.

Alan Truscott, Bridge Editor, New York Times: The best new book to appear in 1980 seems certain to be "Partnership Defense in Bridge."

The author has surveyed a complex and vital field that has been largely neglected in the literature of the game. The player of moderate experience is sure to benefit from the wealth of examples and problems dealing with signaling and other matters relating to cooperation in defense.

And experts who feel they have nothing more to learn neglect this book at their peril: The final test of 20 problems has been presented to some of the country's best partnerships, and non has approached a maximum score.

Bridge World Magazine: As a practical guide for tournament players, no defensive book compares with Kit Woolsey's "Part-

PARTNERSHIP DEFENSE IN BRIDGE BY KIT WOOLSEY

EDITED BY DEANIE YOMTO[?]

nership Defense in Bridge" whi[ch] is by far the best book of its ki[nd] that we have seen. As a techni[cal] work it is superb, and any go[od] player who does not read it will [be] making one of his biggest errors [in] bridge judgment.

The author's theme is partnership cooperation. He believe[s] there are many more points to [be] won through careful play, back[ed] by relatively complete und[er]standings, than through spectacular coups or even through choi[ce] among sensible conventions. [We] agree. If you don't, you will ve[ry] likely change your mind (or [at] least modify the strength of yo[ur] opinion) after reading wh[at] Woolsey has to say.

Published 1980. . .Paperback
**Recommended for: Intermedi[ate]
through expert.**

DO YOU KNOW YOUR PARTNER? by An[dy]
Bernstein and Randy Baron $1.95 A fun-filled qu[iz]
to allow you to really get to know your partner. Som[e] questions concern bridge, some don't — only you ca[n] answer and only your partner can score it. A[n] inexpensive way to laugh yourself to a bette[r] partnership.
Published 1979   paperback
Recommended for: all bridge players.

DEVYN PRESS
151 Thierman Lane
Louisville, KY 40207
(502) 895-1354

OUTSIDE KY. CALL TOLL FREE
1-800-626-1598
FOR VISA / MASTER CARD
ORDERS ONLY

ORDER FORM

**Number
Wanted**

_____ DO YOU KNOW YOUR PARTNER?, Bernstein-Baron . . . . x **$ 1.95** =	_____
_____ COMPLETE BOOK OF OPENING LEADS, Blackwood . . . . x **12.95** =	_____
_____ HAVE I GOT A STORY FOR YOU!, Eber and Freeman . . . . x **7.95** =	_____
_____ THE FLANNERY TWO DIAMOND CONVENTION, Flannery . . . . . x **7.95** =	_____
_____ TABLE TALK, Goodwin . . . . x **5.95** =	_____
_____ THE ART OF LOGICAL BIDDING, Gorski . . . . x **4.95** =	_____
_____ INDIVIDUAL CHAMPIONSHIP BRIDGE SERIES (Please specify) . x **.95** =	_____
_____ BRIDGE CONVENTIONS COMPLETE, Kearse (Paperback) . . . . x **17.95** =	_____
_____ BRIDGE CONVENTIONS COMPLETE, Kearse (Hardcover) . . . . x **24.95** =	_____
_____ 101 BRIDGE MAXIMS, Kelsey . . . . x **7.95** =	_____
_____ DYNAMIC DEFENSE, Lawrence . . . . x **9.95** =	_____
_____ PARTNERSHIP UNDERSTANDINGS, Lawrence . . . . x **2.95** =	_____
_____ PLAY BRIDGE WITH MIKE LAWRENCE, Lawrence . . . . x **9.95** =	_____
_____ WINNING BRIDGE INTANGIBLES, Lawrence and Hanson . . . . . . x **2.95** =	_____
_____ TICKETS TO THE DEVIL, Powell . . . . x **5.95** =	_____
_____ PLAY THESE HANDS WITH ME, Reese . . . . x **7.95** =	_____
_____ BRIDGE: THE BIDDER'S GAME, Rosenkranz . . . . x **12.95** =	_____
_____ MODERN IDEAS IN BIDDING, Rosenkranz-Truscott . . . . x **9.95** =	_____
_____ TEST YOUR PLAY AS DECLARER, VOL. 1, Rubens-Lukacs . . . . . . x **5.95** =	_____
_____ TEST YOUR PLAY AS DECLARER, VOL. 2, Rubens-Lukacs . . . . . . x **5.95** =	_____
_____ DEVYN PRESS BOOK OF BRIDGE PUZZLES #1, Sheinwold . . . . x **4.95** =	_____
_____ DEVYN PRESS BOOK OF BRIDGE PUZZLES #2, Sheinwold . . . . x **4.95** =	_____
_____ DEVYN PRESS BOOK OF BRIDGE PUZZLES, # 3, Sheinwold . . . . . . x **4.95** =	_____
_____ STANDARD PLAYS OF CARD COMBINATIONS FOR CONTRACT	
BRIDGE, Truscott, Gordy and Gordy . . . . x **·6.95** =	_____
_____ PARTNERSHIP DEFENSE, Woolsey . . . . x **8.95** =	_____
_____ MATCHPOINTS, Woolsey . . . . x **9.95** =	_____

*QUANTITY DISCOUNT
ON ABOVE ITEMS:
10% over $25, 20% over $50*

We accept checks, money
orders and VISA or MASTER
CARD. For charge card
orders, send your card number and expiration date.

SUBTOTAL [ ]

LESS QUANTITY DISCOUNT [ ]

TOTAL [ ]

_____ | THE CHAMPIONSHIP BRIDGE SERIES
Vol. I, II, and III . . . . x $9.95 each (No further discount)
All 36 . . . . x 25.95 (No further discount)
[ ]

_____ PLAY IT AGAIN, SAM, Reese and Hoffman . . . . x $7.95 = [ ]

_____ COUNTDOWN TO BETTER BRIDGE, Kelsey . . . . . x $9.95 = [ ]

ADD $1.00
SHIPPING
PER ORDER

TOTAL FOR BOOKS [ ]

SHIPPING ALLOWANCE [ ]

AMOUNT ENCLOSED [ ]

NAME _____

ADDRESS _____

CITY _____ STATE _____ ZIP _____